Shared Governance in Times of Change:

A Practical Guide for Universities and Colleges

By Steven C. Bahls

About AGB

Since 1921, the Association of Governing Boards of Universities and Colleges (AGB) has had one mission: to strengthen and protect this country's unique form of institutional governance through its research, services, and advocacy. Serving more than 1,280 member boards, nearly 2,000 institutions, and 35,000 individuals, AGB is the only national organization providing university and college presidents, board chairs, trustees, and board professionals of both public and private institutions and institutionally related foundations with resources that enhance their effectiveness.

In accordance with its mission, AGB has developed programs and services that strengthen the partnership between the president and governing board; provide guidance to regents and trustees; identify issues that affect tomorrow's decision making; and foster cooperation among all constituencies in higher education. For more information, visit www.agb.org.

About Northern Trust

Northern Trust's dedicated practice—Foundation & Institutional Advisors—is committed to serving midsize nonprofit organizations through sophisticated investment management solutions, strategic insights and world-class resources. Northern Trust's dedicated practice helps each nonprofit achieve its mission by providing administrative and investment oversight of programs, along with award-winning global custody capabilities, planned giving, philanthropic advisory and banking services.

Visit www.northerntrust.com/FIA

Library of Congress Cataloging-in-Publication Data
Bahls, Steven C.
    Shared governance in times of change : a practical guide for universities and colleges / by Steven C. Bahls.
        pages cm
Includes bibliographical references.
    ISBN 978-0-926508-74-3
1. Universities and colleges--United States--Administration. 2. Education, Higher--United States--Administration. 3. Teacher participation in administration--United States. 4. College teachers--United States. 5. Universities and colleges--United States--Faculty. 6. Educational change--United States. I. Title.
LB2341.B253 2014
378.1'01--dc23
                    2014009327

Table of Contents

Foreword

This new publication, *Shared Governance in Times of Change: A Practical Guide for Universities and Colleges,* from Steve Bahls and AGB Press addresses one of higher education's most central—and essential—values. Shared governance has a long history in the sector and, in many ways, defines it.

When I first became involved in higher education, I met with a well-respected president whose first question of me wasn't "What are you doing in this position?" or "What are your priorities?" Instead, he asked, "Who is the most important stakeholder in any college or university?" Before I could respond, he promptly informed me that the only collective body that actually mattered was the faculty. "You can't run a college without the faculty," he explained, "*They* are the ones who matter most." (By the way, I would have given the nod to the faculty had I been allowed to answer.)

Fast forward to a 2009 research study conducted by AGB, *Faculty, Governing Boards, and Institutional Governance.* We wanted to know what faculty and board members knew and thought about each other. What we found was disconcerting: a lack of understanding of each other's roles and limited mutual respect. Such bounded awareness does not serve academic institutions well in meeting the growing demands and expectations of higher education. We need to build a strong, well-traveled bridge between faculties and boards, facilitated by presidents and administrators, to achieve *integral leadership,* as defined in 2006 by AGB's Task Force on the State of the Presidency in American Higher Education.

In seeking to understand shared governance, faculty members often focus on the 1966 AAUP "Statement on Government of Colleges and Universities." Boards often turn to the 2010 "AGB Statement on Board Responsibility for Institutional Governance." While distinct in many ways, they are both grounded in the understanding that the board and the faculty share a commitment to educational quality and results. As those best positioned to facilitate the successful achievement of institutional missions, they must work collaboratively in pursuit those objectives.

Many years have elapsed since that early tutorial about the role of the faculty on campus, and higher education continues to evolve. In today's challenging environment, the process of stakeholder engagement in shaping institutional direction is even more important (and more difficult). Changes to college and university business models, as well as the methodologies and strategies for delivering academic programs, offer new opportunities, present new risks, and call for innovative responses.

Compounding the current challenges of shared governance are faculty structures. Today, roughly 20 percent of faculty members are tenured or on the tenure track. The growing percentage of adjunct faculty members brings to the fore some fundamental questions: What level of faculty engagement in institutional governance is needed for effective academic planning and institutional success? And, how best to make it happen?

Against a backdrop of disruptive change, Steve looks at shared governance through a fresh lens. He examines shared governance in a historic context, reflects on past patterns of board-faculty relations, and suggests practical approaches for going forward. As with many issues related to how the board and the faculty work together, some—many, we hope—readers will find valuable insight and advice in the pages that follow. Others may take issue with the recommendations because they do not extend the hand of engagement sufficiently or because they go too far in sharing governance. Our hope is that this publication reboots the dialogue among boards, presidents, and faculties about the state of shared governance at their college, university, or system because today's environment demands a new way of making decisions.

As fiduciaries, boards are ultimately accountable for institutional policy. However, the stakes are too high to limit meaningful stakeholder engagement. Higher education cannot achieve greater levels of student success unless we recognize that boards, presidents, faculty members, and others should strive for meaningful ways to participate in making the tough decisions that lie ahead. AGB is pleased that such a well-regarded leader in higher education as Steve Bahls was willing to create a roadmap of this complicated new terrain and help us navigate to a better state of shared governance. AGB is thankful to Northern Trust for its generous support of this publication.

Richard D. Legon
President, Association of Governing Boards of Universities and Colleges
March 2014

Preface

The road that stretches before our feet is a challenge to the heart long before it tests the strength of our legs.—St. Thomas Aquinas

I STARTED RESEARCHING AND WRITING THIS BOOK DURING A SUMMER sabbatical in northern Canada. The journey included a rafting expedition on one the great rivers of the North. While we explored these magical lands, seasoned rafting guides taught me two valuable and practical lessons. First, when sinking in the quicksand created by glacial silt, keep moving—rapidly. Second, if you focus too much on mere annoyances, such as hoards of mosquitoes, you won't focus on the big threats—grizzly bears and unexpected whitewater rapids around the bend.

These are valuable lessons for higher education today. Leaders at many institutions feel that they are sinking into quicksand created by disruptive changes in higher education. Many may feel frozen in place, incapable of moving to better ground. At the same time, many boards are focused on the mere annoyances facing them—this complaint or that dispute—and not on the true threats posed, for example, by the growth of alternative models for higher education and challenging economic circumstances and changing student populations. It is time for boards, faculties, and administrations to align their efforts and their goals so they can respond in a timely way to change. And it is time to better use the mechanisms of shared governance to move toward a culture of collective responsibility, looking together over the horizon for tomorrow's opportunities.

There *are* opportunities, but colleges and universities simply cannot move forward without all stakeholders being committed to creative, bold solutions. Because they have a smaller margin for error during challenging economic times than during more economically stable periods, they need to implement decisions more judiciously and expeditiously. The linchpin for doing so is effective shared governance aligning the board, the administration, and the faculty around institutional priorities.

To many, shared governance is the Holy Grail of higher education. It has a long history. During the late medieval period, universities honored academic freedom and faculty governance as a way of establishing needed independence from student guilds, as well as royal and papal authorities. Over time, faculty members individually began to set their own teaching hours and methodology; collectively, they took responsibility for curriculum and teaching qualifications. Early universities in the United States followed the European model of keeping faculty at the center of the academic program, and yet they also created external governing boards. From the early days of American higher education, there has been a struggle to define the respective roles of the faculty, administration, and the governing board.

Shared governance is a concept that few board members, faculty members, or presidents would want to question publicly, although many might question it privately. (The title "president" is used here to refer to all chief executive officers of universities and colleges.) At the same time, it is one of the most misunderstood concepts in higher education because those who believe in its virtues often define it in very different ways, depending upon their vantage points. In my nearly 30 years in higher education, I have found that although the principle is endorsed by most in higher education, only rarely is it successfully and consistently implemented. Commitment to shared governance is often a mile wide and an inch deep. In truth, institutions that are serious about doing the hard work of sharing governance are asking the board, faculty, and president to embark upon a momentous journey—a journey that is likely to be a test of our hearts more than a test of our legs.

When I was a faculty member, conversations in the faculty lounge lamented the breakdown of shared governance. Now I hear conversations at presidents' meetings about conflict between the faculty and boards and the challenges of bringing them together. And conversations in the hallways after board meetings involve board members who are baffled about how to share governance in a way that results in timely decisions. Most of these conversations involve frustrations and disappointments, but not many offer answers or best practices.

Early in my academic career, I taught corporate governance and corporate responsibility courses at the University of Montana School of Law. Never once did I feel the need to mention shared governance. In the framework of the law, it's barely recognized as a legal concept. But when I made the transition to higher-education administration, I quickly learned that shared governance is at the heart of higher education's values and traditions.

I also quickly learned that many view shared governance as a set of fences and boundaries, with useful rules of engagement for when conflict arises. But I hoped for more. Could shared governance be looked at as a vehicle for aligning priorities and generating solutions that were based on or resulted in shared responsibility for the institution as a whole? I found very little to guide my thinking about this broader view of shared governance. I approached the Association of Governing Boards of Universities and Colleges (AGB) about the need for more practical guidance—and was invited to write this book.

I hope it will help faculty leaders, board members, and college and university administrators to understand the difficult concept of shared governance and to use it effectively. The first step is for the faculty, boards, and presidents, based on candid discussions, to move toward a common definition applicable to their particular institution—one that is firmly based in the mission of the institution. Then they should work to understand the barriers to effective shared governance. These barriers, when observed and understood, should be easier to overcome. I offer five overarching practices that can be used to facilitate effective shared governance. And when there is strong shared governance, there should be strong alignment around and commitment to institutional priorities. There may still be some quicksand and an occasional grizzly to cope with, but everyone involved can be working to avoid the quagmires and keep their eyes on the real challenges ahead.

Chapter 1. Why Work for Effective Shared Governance?

The best test of truth is the power of the thought to get itself accepted in the competition of the market...—Justice Oliver Wendell Holmes, Jr., dissenting opinion in *Abrams v. United States* (1919)

SAYING THAT HIGHER EDUCATION IS ON THE CUSP OF TRANSFORMATIVE change tends to illicit little response, as we have been hearing this urgent message for more than a decade. Yet, the case cannot be understated, regardless of how often it is expressed. Sweeping change demands significant innovation developed from the best ideas. The many challenges facing higher education today involve shifting demographics, spiraling costs, and the rise of new ways to provide postsecondary education—greater use of technology, new types of certifications beyond traditional degrees, new providers, for example. For most traditional colleges and universities, I would argue that the "enemy within" in responding to disruptive change is ineffective governance.

Implementing timely change in challenging circumstances requires leaders willing and able to innovate in ways not traditionally seen in higher education. It is not sufficient for such leadership to come just from presidents and board leaders, however. Faculty leaders need to become more innovative and effective in developing programs that will lead to the learning outcomes demanded of today's students and recent graduates. Yet misalignment of focus and priorities among the president, the board, and the faculty over the direction and pace of change often lies behind inadequate responses to challenges. Whether the college is four-year or two-year, private or public, traditional or specialized, many faculties are increasingly at odds with the administration and the board over the institution's direction—whether over spending priorities, use of technology, adding or closing programs, building or acquiring new campuses, changing the mix of faculty from tenure-track to adjunct, or the like.

Especially in today's environment, shared governance is hard work. It is messy work. But the alternative is shared blame and the risk of inaction. Commitments to share governance often backfire by unduly raising expectations among those hoping to participate in running the institution. Those disappointed by decisions made after bungled efforts to share governance often simply walk away from the table, sometimes preferring to take the easier route of undermining the institution's collective process of decision making. Such broken systems may lead to acrimony among constituencies, making effective shared governance even more difficult.

Why should boards, administrators, and the faculty undertake this hard work and risk failure? Because the hard work can pay huge dividends. And because the cost of not changing to meet today's and tomorrow's challenges is too high.

THE TURMOIL

Clayton Christensen, author of *The Innovator's Dilemma* and professor at the Harvard Business School, has written persuasively that American colleges and universities are experiencing a seismic shift involving both its spiraling cost and the rise of new economic models for higher education. As have other commentators, he argues that there is doubt about whether traditional institutions in American higher education can adapt fast enough to address the new set of external circumstances.

The trends currently pressuring many institutions are numerous and diverse:

- From the White House and Congress to major foundations to editorial boards of the nation's best newspapers, we hear constant calls for more institutional accountability, better career outcomes, and lower costs.
- In many parts of the country, particularly the Northeast and Midwest, the number of high-school graduates is declining, with obvious implications for freshman classes.
- The academic workforce is continuing to change, with more courses being taught by part-time and non-tenure-track faculty members who are probably less invested in the long-term success of the institution or less available for administrative committee work.

- Liberal arts colleges and humanities departments at universities have generally seen an enrollment dip, with students and their families wondering about the practicality of these majors in a career-oriented world.

- The government is putting pressure on colleges and universities to offer credit for competency-based experience.

- Crumbling infrastructures plague many institutions that have long lists of deferred maintenance projects.

- The borders of campuses are more porous. Many students today transfer from institution to institution and yet ultimately fail to complete degrees.

- Using online courses to substitute for or supplement traditional classroom-based courses, as well as unbundling majors and degrees into certificates and other non-degree designations, can fundamentally change the relationship between the faculty and the administration.

SHARED GOVERNANCE DURING DISRUPTIVE TIMES

Board members, faculty leaders, and presidents understand that they need to respond, but many have not developed strategies for how to do so effectively. Board members are typically out front in urging aggressive strategies because they have experienced similar disruptive changes in their businesses or within other organizations. Faculty members wonder how this will affect them, fearing that disruptive change will affect the values they hold dear and their jobs. Presidents and chancellors are deeply concerned but grapple with how to create the alignment among all constituencies required to develop the capacities to respond.

Successful businesses understand that they can't be good at everything, can't be all things to all people, and can't continue to succeed without evolving. Colleges and universities must take the same approach. Strategic plans can no longer be a laundry list of every constituency's wants and desires. Rather, colleges and universities must focus on how to build value by achieving the outcomes demanded by students at a cost they can afford or by making tough choices, such as cutting programs or reducing expenses in a meaningful way. This requires inclusively debated and clearly communicated decisions regarding

institutional priorities and resources. Some observers would say that reve-
nue-driven decision making has trumped mission-driven decision making at
many campuses. Yet agreement on mission can be a uniting force that aligns
actions and brings together the stakeholders in shared governance.

Directing and conducting such discussions to arrive at mission-driven
outcomes requires what AGB has defined as *integral leadership*, which "links
the president, the faculty, and the board in a well-functioning partnership
purposefully devoted to a well-defined, broadly affirmed institutional vision"
(*The Leadership Imperative,* 2006).

THE GOALS OF SHARED GOVERNANCE

The advantages of sharing governance can be oversimplified. Boards may
consider the benefits to be creating buy-in from the faculty for board decisions.
Faculty members may see the benefit to be having a seat at the table with board
members to ensure that the board understands their point of view.

But these narrow approaches sell the many benefits of shared governance
short. Boards that view shared governance as a way to gain buy-in are likely to
view shared governance as little more than a formality or an additional hoop to
be jumped through in decision making, without doing the hard work of actually
aligning their priorities for the institution with those of the faculty. Faculty
members who view shared governance as an opportunity to be at the table to
persuade board members to see things their way are unlikely to be ready for the
hard and sustained work of consensus building.

Exhibit 1: The Goals of Shared Governance

Ability to address new challenges | Better-informed, timely decisions | Faster, more effective implementation | Mutual investment in outcomes | More satisfying participation in governance | Model of civility

Shared governance must move colleges and universities beyond the traditional model, which seeks to find short-term political solutions to the differing views. This model allows the faculty and the board to function independently by creating fences and boundaries around authority. Instead, leadership in disruptive times should be about aggressive steps to identify and implement sustainable strategic directions through aligning the interests of stakeholders in a shared academic vision.

The hard work and the risks of sharing governance, however, are justified by six important and tangible results.

Ability to Address New Challenges

Effective shared governance can produce a system in which board members, faculty members, and administrators can develop bold strategic priorities that respond to serious challenges and tomorrow's realities. Specifically, it can produce the following:

- **A shared understanding of the deep consequences of transformative change.** Before institutions make necessary changes to remain sustainable, they must develop a common understanding of the challenges they face. Effective planning simply cannot take place in a vacuum.

- **A shared sense of urgency.** Institutional leaders need a common understanding of the urgency of change. If they believe that the challenges will go away as the economy improves or the institution's endowment grows, they will not be ready to take bold strategic steps. Or, if institutional leaders believe a narrow approach such as marketing the institution more effectively is the way to respond to questions about their operations or priorities, they will not develop the strategic directions needed, within the context of their mission, to remain sustainable in changing times.

- **A shared commitment to do strategic planning in a timely way.** Ad hoc, fragmented plans—or plans developed to resolve only the most immediate and annoying problems in an institution—are not the answer. A common understanding of the value of planning as a way of anticipating and responding to external and internal change can lead to a shared commitment to develop commonly accepted and bold solutions to deeper problems.

- **A shared commitment to implement strategic plans in a sustained and timely way.** When institutions create alignment of priorities through open, participative, and robust planning processes, all parties are likely to have sufficient investment in the plans to undertake the hard work of implementing them. Implementation of a strategic plan for many institutions *will* involve difficult actions—for example, reducing the number of employees, terminating or scaling back programs, changing how people do their jobs on a day-to-day basis. There will be resistance to many of these changes at many levels within the institution. Developing a shared commitment to take the hard actions necessary will help institutional leaders withstand the inevitable pushback.

- **A deep pool of trust, understanding, and goodwill.** When constituencies work together to align their sense of mission and strategic direction, they can build the trust and understanding needed to sustain them when strategic planning does not go exactly as expected. Aligned priorities are not an insurance policy against disagreement, but reaching them should have created the trust and goodwill among leaders that allow them to get through disagreements.

Better-Informed, Timely Decisions

Effective shared governance leading to collaborative decision making gives colleges and universities the potential to make higher-quality, better-informed decisions that support sustainable institutions. Shared governance provides a measure of insurance against precipitous decision making. When multiple constituencies are at the table, there is a greater probability that in-depth analysis will take place. Issues are easier to identify, assumed facts are probed more deeply, tentative solutions are more fully vetted, and those implementing the decisions provide more analysis as to the possible unintended consequences of the decision.

Indeed, there is no better way to generate essential input, critical thinking, and hard questions than involving faculty members in key discussions early in the decision-making process. Boards engaging all constituencies in candid discussions are more likely to develop keen insight into how things are and how things might be. By disposition, board members are trained to ask probing questions, while faculty members are skeptical but still accustomed to asking important questions in the classroom and in their research. This combination sets the stage for deliberate, thoughtful, and high-quality decision making. It creates a "marketplace of ideas" that can lead to better, mission-focused decisions.

On occasion, board members or administrators may push for risky "grand solutions" instead of the more nuanced solutions that faculty members might suggest. This seems to be more common recently, as boards are more genuinely concerned by the advent of alternative models of delivery and the economic pressures on higher education. In the book *How the Mighty Fall: And Why Some Companies Never Give In,* author Jim Collins (also author of *Good to Great)* argues that the businesses he studied that adopted grand, bet-the-farm solutions were those most likely to fail because the organizations strayed from core competencies and were unable to master new competencies quickly enough. The marketplace of ideas created by effective shared governance critically analyzes these go-for-broke solutions and encourages exploration of other bold, but less risky, alternatives.

A criticism of shared governance is that it leads to solutions made by committee that look like three-humped camels when the committee involved was charged with designing a horse. A corollary to this criticism is that shared governance risks making unwise concessions to the change-averse. When shared governance yields these results, it is probably because those responsible for shared governance misunderstood that the goal of shared governance is not consensus but, instead, the best possible decision.

Different Perspectives, Collaborative Result

At Augustana College, we have used shared governance to appropriately respond to the greater focus by both our nation's leaders and our students on graduation rates and post-graduation career placement. Our constituencies together identified improving job placement rates as a key strategic priority. At first, board members believed the solution was a more robust career center. But faculty members pointed out that career advising often starts with them, as they help graduate and undergraduate students understand career options for different majors, arrange for internships, and connect with alumni who might assist with career development.

Many faculty members, however, observed they did not have the time or knowledge to be as effective as they would like to be with career advice. Administrators, who had better access to data, noted that those academic areas whose graduates reported the least satisfaction with their education tended to be larger departments, where students do not advance through their studies in cohorts. The solution, endorsed by all, was to create "career communities" of alumni, faculty members, and career-development professionals for each major to help students find internships and first jobs. These differing perspectives enabled the board to work with the administration in applying resources to support tactical solutions that the entire community owns—the faculty, coaches, student-activities staff, and residential-life staff—and to have a greater career focus across each major.

Faster, More Effective Implementation

For-profit universities have the luxury of a hierarchical way of making decisions, which substantially cuts implementation time. Early adopters of new ideas usually have the competitive advantage. Yet traditional approaches to shared governance often emphasize developing consensus before decisions are implemented. Identifying student-learning outcomes gets bogged down in drawn-out committee discussions. Major curricular modifications tend to take several years, with assumptions debated anew each academic year during the course of the revisions. But these ill-defined timetables for making decisions are unacceptable for higher education today.

Contrary to conventional wisdom, shared governance can speed the time from identifying a problem to implementing tactics to resolve it. While more time may be spent debating the issue and considering strategies and tactics, once there is ownership of aligned strategies, it is easier, and often quicker, to develop and carry out the tactics for agreed-upon strategies.

Why is this the case? Because shared governance works with and respects faculty culture. The late A. Bartlett Giamatti, a past president of Yale, captured the essence of this culture when he said: "University professors never think of themselves as employees; they think of themselves as the heart of the place, as the texture of the place, as the essence of the place." (*A Free and Ordered Space: The Real World of the University,* 1989, p.43). Giamatti was right. Our most important constituencies, our students and graduates, view the faculty as the heart and soul of our institutions. Thus having faculty members ready to support solutions to problems can improve and speed implementation.

Solutions in Six Months

When the recession of 2008 hit, many institutions missed their enrollment targets. While most institutions were strong enough to take a one-year hit in the size of the entering class, a two-year hit would be a much larger problem. To try to get their enrollment numbers back up, several colleges looked at research that demonstrated that an increasing number of prospective students were going to their second-choice colleges because the colleges that otherwise would have been their first choice did not have the programs or majors they wanted.

Because of the trust and agreement on priorities between the board and faculty, one institution's board established a fund to create new majors and programs designed to attract students. The fund was made possible by donations from board members. The faculty and administrators worked together to propose six new majors and two new NCAA Division III sports, all within six months. Faculty leaders responded to the urgency of maintaining robust enrollment because of the trust built by sharing governance. For each of the next several years, the institution was able to enroll record numbers of new first-year students, in large part because of these new programs.

The process of working together at this institution to overcome the challenges posed by the recession was possible because this institution, a year earlier, worked deliberately to set the stage for a strategic-planning process to further align the strategic priorities of the board, president, and faculty.

Mutual Investment in Outcomes

Institutions that move beyond boundaries set by traditional shared governance to a culture that aligns the board, faculty, and administration in developing better solutions have a competitive advantage. When faculty members and board members align their strategic directions and faculty members are fully invested in those directions, it is much more likely sustained changes will result.

When shared governance works effectively in public and private institutions, faculty members take a deeper personal interest in the challenges facing the institution. They tend to invest more of their career there, instead of moving to a different institution when a position opens with better compensation. Faculty members who have a sense of ownership typically have greater levels of job satisfaction, making for better teaching and better academic leadership.

Of course, accountability measures are also important. Periodic reviews of the impact of implemented changes should also be part of any strategic plan involving innovation. A sense of investment in the institution is important but so is the knowledge that people will be held accountable in carrying out strategic directions.

Institutions should be sensitive to barriers and address those that interfere with the faculty engagement necessary for mutual investment in outcomes. These barriers often include limited faculty engagement in faculty governance, a focus on the interest of departments or disciplines over the whole of the college, and reward systems that do not encourage faculty engagement in governance. (See Chapter 4.)

More Satisfying Participation in Governance

Effective shared governance makes board service more satisfying. Many college presidents try to meet personally every year or two with individual board members to find out how they view their service to the institution. The comment they often hear, and most like to hear, is that service on the college's board is the most satisfying of any board to which they belong. Satisfied board members who are alumni tend to mention the ability to give back to an institution that was formative for them and to prize the ability to serve a new generation of students.

But board service is not satisfying for all, and some may not embrace shared governance. In a 2009 AGB survey, only half of the presidents described the relationship between the faculty and their board as good or positive (Schwartz et al., *Faculty, Governing Boards, and Institutional Governance,* 2009). Many presidents and board members expressed deep frustration with the difference in cultures among the board, faculty, and administration and confusion about their respective roles in the overall governance of the institution. When shared governance is not working, presidents find it immeasurably more difficult and less pleasant to move the institution forward, and board service becomes a burden.

When the relationship between the board and the faculty is viewed as adversarial, it is often because there is no structure to allow for the candid and regular interactions necessary to build trust and confidence between them. As board and faculty members develop relationships through shared endeavors, a board member may be invited to guest lecture at a class or meet informally with students about career development. Board members' connections with faculty serve as a way to identify promising recent graduates who might be great employees. And simple things like conversations over dinner allow board members to reconnect with the special mission of the institution. Just as satisfied faculty members make for a better institution, satisfied board members make for a better institution. Board members' service to their institutions will be viewed not as an obligation or duty but rather may be seen as a privilege and part of their life's calling.

Similarly, service as a faculty member is much more satisfying when shared governance works effectively. Faculty members want to have as much control over their work as possible. To the extent they are respected by the board and president, listened to, and considered a vital part of decision making, they tend to have greater job satisfaction because they feel a sense of control over their own destinies. Just as board members may enjoy getting to know faculty members, faculty members may enjoy interacting with board members. Faculty members and board members are more similar than might first be imagined. In addition to their passion for the institution, they are critical and creative thinkers and focused on making a better future for students.

Model of Civility

Effective shared governance provides a model of civility and a sense of shared purpose. When governance is not effective, students, alumni, and donors see it. Many faculty members are not shy about taking their frustrations over decisions to their students or even to the student newspaper or local press. Similarly, some faculty members increasingly use widely accessible blogs to share their frustrations. Students may pick up and amplify this frustration.

Conversely, effective governance is usually evident, too. Faculty members are closer to students and some alumni than many board members and administrators. So when faculty can explain and endorse a difficult decision, the institution is strengthened. When alumni and students question unpopular decisions, it helps if faculty members can explain the decision instead of simply shaking their heads and blaming the administration and the board.

Students observe how disagreements are handled on campus, which they may view as a model for how to resolve disagreements and how to make difficult decisions after they graduate. When controversial decisions are followed by immature or inappropriate behavior, students may be more likely to see this as a legitimate response. But if students see highly participatory ways of decision making (including the opportunity for them to participate at some level), they may be more inclined to adopt more productive types of decision making in their own professional and personal lives.

Broken Shared Governance: A Tale of a College

With one year under his belt, the new president of a nationally ranked liberal arts college had a difficult budget to balance. Faculty morale was at an all-time low. Shared governance had clearly broken down by the time the faculty senate passed a vote asking the president to resign. Then, it went from bad to worse. Someone created a Web site and posted confidential documents, including personal e-mails and minutes of private meetings that lambasted the president. Observing the faculty vilifying the president in op-eds and blog posts, a few students posted videos online in which they encouraged the president to not take this personally, offered him cookies to show their compassion, and then joined in the vitriolic attacks. The campus disagreements became the subject of local and national press coverage. Because shared governance had broken down, normal channels of communication also broke down. Students and faculty members explained that the public Web site was their most effective tool in communicating their concerns to the board and president. But the antics made everyone (board, president, faculty, and students) look foolish, and the college had difficulty recruiting students and faculty members for the next year. Perhaps most disappointingly, no one on campus modeled the kind of critical thinking and constructive debate that a liberal arts education is supposed to inspire.

CONCLUSION

Times of change create ambiguity and uncertainty, which often sows the seeds of tension and turmoil. Now, more than ever, institutions of higher education need a holistic approach to resolving difficult decisions. Boards, presidents, and faculty must develop a constructive way of reaching agreement around critical issues and challenges and then working collectively on sustainable solutions. An effective process for making decisions has three elements: (1) the context and environment in which the decision is made, (2) the culture of the institution and its structures of authority, and (3) substance of the issue itself.

When shared governance is understood and practiced as a system for identifying and aligning priorities, institutions will be able to move through moments of friction more smoothly. Shared governance can—and should— provide boards, faculty, and administrators with a way of working collabora- tively toward a common vision. But no single recipe for shared governance can guarantee success, and making it work requires hard work. Together, the board, the president, and the faculty of each institution must design and support a system for moving together in the same direction.

Chapter 2. Competing Views of Shared Governance

My apple trees will never get across
And eat the cones under his pines, I tell him.
He only says, "Good fences make good neighbors."
Spring is the mischief in me, and I wonder
If I could put a notion in his head:
"Why do they make good neighbors? Isn't it
Where there are cows?"
But here there are no cows.
—Robert Frost, Mending Wall

WHENEVER ANYONE RAISES THE TOPIC OF SHARED GOVERNANCE WITH me, I ask the individual what he or she means by the term. The responses are most always different. Indeed, the biggest barrier to effective shared governance is failure to understand and agree on the definition and how it should be put into action. Because there is no commonly accepted definition, even those faculty members, administrators, and board members who sincerely aspire to share governance are too often disappointed with the process. Worse yet, because of their varying views and cultures, these stakeholders are likely to become frustrated, viewing the other parties' commitments to shared governance as insincere. Too frequently, parties withdraw from patient and effective participation in the process.

This chapter is designed to serve as a vehicle for boards, faculties, and administrators to consider different views of shared governance. As readers consider how they themselves would define shared governance, they can also assess how various constituencies at their institutions would define and practice it and whether there are ways to align the various definitions. (See Appendix: Shared Governance Survey.) But most important, as stakeholders work to develop a common understanding of shared governance at their institution, they should ask whether the model will help their institutions satisfy the six goals in Exhibit 1.

The three most traditional perspectives on shared governance, summarized briefly in this chapter, do not fully satisfy these goals, nor do they reflect AGB's perspective on shared governance. This chapter proposes a fourth perspective: viewing shared governance as a process to align priorities among faculty, boards, and presidents. While not perfect, it does a much better job of allowing an institution to meet the objectives required for moving from simply sharing governance to sharing responsibility for an institution's future.

THREE TRADITIONAL (AND INADEQUATE) PERSPECTIVES ON SHARED GOVERNANCE

Over the past 50 years, the views of presidents and board members regarding shared governance seem to have fallen into three general categories. Each perspective, by itself, is inadequate to address today's realities in higher education and the need to respond in a timely and effective way to disruptive change.

Shared Governance as Equal Rights to Governance

In this outmoded view, shared governance ensures that the faculty, board, and administration have equal say in all governance matters, including budgets, academic directions of the institution, and strategic planning. No decisions are made until a consensus is reached by all. This model, while attractive in theory, is problematic under the law and in practice. Because it effectively gives the faculty veto power over decisions within the board's primary fiduciary responsibility and gives boards veto power over matters commonly recognized to be primarily within faculty responsibility, it is a sure formula for indecision, deadlock, and even hostility.

State laws, as well as best practices, require the boards of all nonprofit organizations—in meeting their fiduciary responsibilities—to act with care in their stewardship of the organization. Boards have the ultimate authority within colleges and universities. While boards may delegate the power to accomplish certain tasks, boards can't do so blindly. Laws in all 50 states provide that the board has a duty to exercise a high level of care and ultimate responsibility for the institution, even for those tasks they delegate. Failure to make needed and important decisions is a violation of the board's duty of care. The duty of care that boards have for institutions is discussed in detail in Chapter 3.

University and college boards are ultimately responsible under state law for all aspects of their institutions, including policies involving teaching and learning. The Association of Governing Boards provides more detailed guidance to institutions about basic governing-board responsibilities in its publication *Effective Governing Boards*. Among other responsibilities, boards must oversee strategic planning, fiscal integrity, and educational quality and must ensure institutional autonomy and academic freedom.

It is appropriate that boards delegate primary responsibility for academic standards and academic programs to the president and the faculty. They should ensure educational quality by informing themselves about important aspects of the educational program and then holding the administration and faculty accountable for ensuring that student-learning outcomes are achieved and measured. Including the faculty in decision making began with the practical need to have the right expertise at the table. In the early days of American higher education, when most presidents were clergy, it was clear that they didn't know everything, or even much of anything, about many disciplines. Thus faculty members' input on curriculum and their responsibility for teaching were crucial. That is no less true today. Thus boards should exercise their right to overrule core academic decisions very sparingly.

A variation of this equal-rights view of shared governance is that the board, the administration, and the faculty should wait to make decisions until they can develop a consensus. But that may produce ineffective decisions— crafted to please each constituency but without integrity. Horse-trading in higher education (for example, we will keep this unproductive program if you consent to eliminating that other one) is not the way to make the bold decisions required today.

Hard and Soft Governance

Robert Birnbaum, professor emeritus of higher education at the University of Maryland, College Park, observes that there are really two types of college and university governance. One is "hard" governance, which "refers to the structure, regulation, and systems of sanction in organizations that define authority relationships." The other is "soft" governance, which "encompasses the systems of social connections and interactions in an organization that help to develop and maintain individual and group norms."

Birnbaum is correct when he states that "while hard governance can channel and to some extent harness the power of soft governance so that the two are mutually reinforcing, in and of itself, it appears to have little influence." He notes, "hard governance makes little difference because most of the important decisions made in the university occur outside the formal systems." Although boards approve programs of study, faculty members determine what to teach and students determine what and whether to learn. Without shared governance, soft governance could trump hard governance, leading to individual domains and little alignment of priorities.

Systems of hard governance and soft governance are aligned when the systems of social connections and interactions support the decisions made by systems of hard governance. Systems of shared governance can provide the foundation for this alignment.

Source: Robert Birnbaum, "The End of Shared Governance: Looking Ahead or Looking Back," in William G. Tierney and Vicente M. Lechuga, eds., *Restructuring Shared Governance in Higher Education* (San Francisco: Jossey-Bass, 2004).

Faculty cultures and board cultures are fundamentally different, making consensus on each and every issue difficult to achieve. Unlike businesses, where partners have a common interest in maximizing profits, the concerns, interests, and priorities of faculty and board members are not so easily aligned. Faculty members tend to be more concerned with the quality of the student-learning experience than whether the budget is met. Board members, as fiduciaries, need to be concerned about both but tend to place a much greater emphasis on budget matters than faculty members do.

Shared Governance as Consultation

In this incomplete view, shared governance requires nothing more than for the party responsible for making decisions to consult with others. Board members and presidents often view shared governance as an obligation to consult with the faculty before major decisions are made, acknowledging that faculty members are closer to many issues than are board members. They assume that if faculty views are considered and if faculty members sometimes "see their fingerprints" on decisions, they are more apt to buy into the decisions and work with the board to implement them.

But consultation alone is not sufficient for effective shared governance. Even though they have been consulted, many faculty members are prone to feel they have not been listened to if decisions do not go their way. Further, for matters at the heart of the academic program, faculty members do not want to simply be consulted—they believe that they have full authority for decisions.

Even outside of academic programs, faculty members may expect a greater role than mere consultation. They may expect to be involved early in the process of decision making on a wide variety of institutional policy issues— when strategic directions are being discussed, not merely after the train has left the station. And because faculty members see shared governance as more than *pro forma* consultation, they want to see that their input has actually helped shape solutions. Too often, boards and presidents ask faculty members for their input but then dismiss it as uninformed or even naïve. Assuming that faculty members will support decisions simply because they've been consulted is viewed as demeaning by most faculty members. And when faculty members feel their views are not respected, they're likely to withdraw from other, more meaningful efforts to share governance. Mere consultation, when substituted for the hard work of building trust and common understandings, does not lead to sustainable and shared priorities. This view of shared governance as consultation encourages the faculty to be reactive to board initiatives, not proactive and entrepreneurial in taking responsibility for addressing tomorrow's realities.

Likewise, boards are charged by law and by best practice with meaningful oversight of the institution, including its academic programs. In practice,
boards delegate to the president (and chief academic officer) responsibility
for working with the faculty to ensure that learning is assessed, deficiencies
monitored, and results improved. Presidents, chief academic officers, and
faculty leaders who provide perfunctory information about academic concerns
to the board under the guise of consulting with the board, do not allow the
board to fulfill its responsibility for ensuring education quality. Boards must
be more than simply consulted; they must be actively involved in ensuring that
policies and practices are in place to promote educational quality.

Shared Governance as Rules of Engagement

In this model, shared governance is a set of rules about the various
roles and authority of the board, faculty, and administration in such things as
academic decisions, budget decisions, selection of the president, and other
operational decisions. But seeing shared governance as creating boundaries
and rules of engagement does not lead to the give and take among the faculty,
president, and board that builds high-quality, timely decisions. Boundaries
create territories where people tend to focus on the past, and they do not
encourage the cross-fertilization necessary for bold and entrepreneurial
approaches that create shared responsibility for moving institutions forward.

Some observers see tension between faculty culture, administrative
culture, and board culture as inescapable. Because there is also tension
between state law, which holds boards responsible for all aspects of their
institutions, and academic tradition, which yields major responsibility for the
academic program to the president, chief academic officer, and faculty, they
believe that this tension needs to be managed through establishing boundaries,
with rules of engagement for when boundaries overlap. Those viewing shared
governance as a defined set of boundaries often cite the "Statement of
Government of Colleges and Universities," adopted in 1966 by the American
Association of University Professors, discussed further in Chapter 3. Although
this statement is nearly 50 years old at this writing, it is still seen by many

Exhibit 2. Shared Governance: Goals and Perspectives

Shared governance as...				
	Equal rights	Consultation	Rules of engagement	System for aligning priorities
Ability to address new challenges	Sacrifices flexibility and risks impasse during times of changes	Allows board to frame forward-looking issues, but does not achieve real faculty engagement	Perpetuates focus on discrete issues as defined by boundaries from the past	**Focuses on holistic, strategic directions for the future**
Better-informed, more timely decisions	Increases time to reach decisions and encourages "three-humped camel" compromises	Fosters information sharing, which leads to better decisions	Provides checks and balances, but does not create a shared sense of direction	**Features transparency, which improves the quality of decisions**
Faster, more effective implementation	Shortens implementation once decision is reached	Slows implementation because a lack of participation in decision making	Establishes a process for implementation	**Requires more frequent interaction, which may slow decision making but speed implementation**
Mutual investment in outcomes	Supports alignment because decisions are not made until consensus is reached, but consensus may be difficult to achieve	Provides information but does not necessarily garner support for outcomes	Has credibility with faculty, so responsibility for results are more likely to be shared	**Builds mutual commitment because outcomes are jointly developed**
More satisfying participation in governance	Confuses the respective responsibilities of the board, president, and faculty	Overlooks importance of stakeholder involvement	Has credibility with faculty	**Brings board and faculty together around passion for the institution**
Model of civility	Supports democratic principles, but may encourage political gamesmanship	Discourages participatory leadership	Focuses on boundaries in authority, which may lead to fragmentation	**Demonstrates that collaborative leadership yields better results**

faculty members as the most important statement of how faculties, boards, and administrations share governance.

The recent spate of faculty no-confidence votes in presidents, and sometimes boards, illustrates the limitations of the statement's approach focused on setting boundaries and rules of engagement. Many no-confidence votes arise in cases of failures of shared governance. Although the reasons for these votes are often attributed to a perceived lack of communication and transparency by the president's office, as well as a perception of an imperial attitude, a closer examination in many cases reveals that what underlies these votes is disagreement about who decides what at the institution, accompanied by deep disagreement as to its direction. While the statement helps set operating procedures, its approach of defining rules of engagement when there is deep disagreement among constituencies has not been sufficient to prevent governance crises at some institutions.

Rules of engagement, from my experience as both an attorney and a college president, do not always lead to open communication. They are helpful for determining how day-to-day decisions are made but are less helpful when an institution is addressing planning and institutional direction. In those cases, fences neither facilitate debate nor make good neighbors. Boards, presidents, and the faculty must get beyond a rulebook and develop an approach that truly aligns priorities, measures outcomes, and holds each other accountable.

A NEW PERSPECTIVE: SHARED GOVERNANCE AS A SYSTEM OF ALIGNING PRIORITIES

The first three views of shared governance may describe how many boards, faculty, and presidents think of shared governance, but each has its shortcomings with respect to producing the united, shared leadership needed to meet today's challenges. Those views of shared governance are not likely to create fertile ground for various constituencies to align their strategies. Nor do these approaches typically encourage bold, innovative, and entrepreneurial solutions. What is needed is a systems approach in which faculty, board members, and administrators actively engage to share responsibility for identifying and pursuing an aligned set of mission-driven sustainable outcomes and priorities. Exhibit 2 summarizes how these different perspectives meet the goals and demands of shared governance, as outlined in Chapter 1.

Shared governance as a system for alignment has two primary parts. The first part is a system for creating alignment of stakeholders on issues of *institutional direction* by developing common understandings of the challenges the institution faces. Common understandings facilitate alignment. And alignment, when systems are properly structured, helps move beyond fragmentation to sustainable strategic directions based on shared responsibility for outcomes. The second part is a system of checks and balances for decisions regarding *operational issues* such as academic programs, tenure and promotion policies, budgeting, and student life. This second part is often guided by the provisions of AGB's "Statement on Board Responsibility for Institutional Governance" and by faculty handbooks.

Consistent with AGB's focus on integral leadership, this fourth perspective of shared governance as a system to align priorities does exactly this through the processes of open, informed, and fair discussion, and through developing shared strategies. Specific tactics for addressing these strategies are then delegated to those responsible for implementing them. Institutions of higher education must seek alignment on the triple priorities of excellent student-learning outcomes, affordability, and financial sustainability.

> "Integral leadership links the president, faculty, and board in a well-functioning partnership purposefully devoted to a well-defined, broadly affirmed institutional vision." (*The Leadership Imperative*, AGB, 2006)

Shared Governance and Sharing Students

At one college, the chair of the board's academic affairs committee felt strongly that more college-bound students were starting at community colleges, and thus that the administration should work to increase the number of community-college transfer students and to permit them to transfer with a greater number of credits. Faculty members, on the other hand, believed that the curriculum they had developed was based on students spending four years at the college. If the board, faculty, and administration had viewed shared governance as equal rights, no action would have been taken to ease transfer restrictions because the faculty would have effectively vetoed it. But this institution viewed shared governance as a way to align priorities.

To do so in this case, board members, administrators, and faculty engaged in joint discussions of the issue. Faculty members asked how transfers fared and, after researching the issue, the administration found that transfer students who had earned an associate's degree from a community college achieved graduation rates equal to or better than transfers from four-year colleges. But transfer students who had not earned an associate's degree fared worse. The faculty, which by its tradition determined which community college credits transferred, agreed that the chief academic officer should then negotiate six pilot agreements with well-respected community colleges to ease the transfer process for students earning an associate's degree. This compromise was possible because faculty and board members aligned their focus on what was best for student-graduation rates.

COMPONENTS OF A SYSTEMS APPROACH TO SHARED GOVERNANCE

There are four important components to building the systems approach:

- Build and maintain a culture of transparency and three-way open communication.
- Foster a shared commitment to jointly consider difficult issues, especially those associated with change, and then jointly develop strategic directions.
- Develop a shared commitment to forward-looking measures of success.
- Implement a system of effective checks and balances to ensure that the institution remains mission-focused.

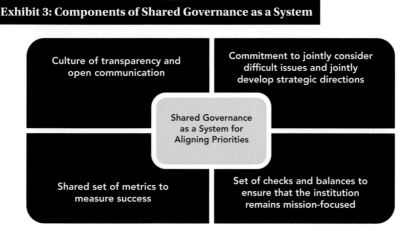

Exhibit 3: Components of Shared Governance as a System

Culture of transparency and open communication

Commitment to jointly consider difficult issues and jointly develop strategic directions

Shared Governance as a System for Aligning Priorities

Shared set of metrics to measure success

Set of checks and balances to ensure that the institution remains mission-focused

A Culture of Transparency and Open Communication

Shared governance, at its best, is based on a culture of open communication among faculty, administrators, and board members. Open communication requires all parties to be transparent with each other. Presidents sometimes withhold information to avoid disappointing or causing discomfort to others. Faculty members can avoid being transparent under the theory that the academic program is theirs and providing information might threaten their independence. Further, on many campuses there may not be mechanisms for direct contact by faculty leaders with board members. And board members may assume that faculty members simply don't have the interest or knowledge to understand, let alone participate in, dealing with a complex issue such as the finances of the college or university. Without transparency and clear communication, shared governance will not work. If different constituencies have access to different sets of information, they cannot be expected to develop common priorities. (For further discussion, see Chapter 6.)

A Commitment to Jointly Consider Difficult Issues and Jointly Develop Strategic Directions

It is not possible to develop common priorities if the board, the faculty, and the administration are only involved in the daily operational issues of shared governance. Rather, each constituency must be more deliberate in considering the critical and difficult new and evolving issues facing the

System-Wide Shared Governance

Effective shared governance is also important within statewide, public systems, but it functions somewhat differently. In many states, important academic policies are made at the system level, by the chancellor and board of regents. Often, parameters for general education are made at the system level, with individual universities responsible for developing more specific programs. Parameters for authorizing new programs, degrees, and majors are also set at the systems level, with system approval required for new programs.

University systems approach shared governance differently from state to state. In states like California, New York, and Maryland, which have a strong centralized system that maintains significant control of academic programs, it is common to have a system-wide academic senate or academic council comprised of faculty members elected from the various universities in the system. In these states, system-wide academic policies are best made only after consultation with the system-wide faculty body. System-wide faculty senates or councils also monitor shared governance at each of the universities and issue public reports on their findings. As William "Brit" Kirwan, chancellor of the University System of Maryland, notes, "Organizational success over the long haul depends on a sense of collaboration at the policy level." He does not take a policy touching on academics to the system board without first consulting with the system-wide faculty council.

Robert Caret, chancellor of the University of Massachusetts System, explains, "We believe that higher education in the United States is the strongest and best in the world, and it has occurred with shared governance as a cornerstone." In states like Massachusetts, where the locus of academic decision making is more clearly at the university level, there is typically no system-wide faculty senate. Caret ensures that there are more informal mechanisms for consulting with faculty, including regular meetings among system leaders, university provosts, and faculty senate chairs.

In other, even more decentralized states, there is no chancellor and university presidents report directly to the state board of regents. In such states, shared governance may be honored by giving faculty leaders the right to speak to issues at the board of regents level.

institution. These constituencies should ask what the institution wants to be and why before trying to develop the strategies and tactics to achieve those objectives. This approach is particularly important to faculty members, who tend to view themselves as the keepers of the mission and traditions of the institution. If discussions forgo the step of asking what the institution is or wants to be, as defined by mission in the context of tomorrow's likely realities, the discussion of what to do will be a rudderless exercise that lacks the integrity required of integral leadership.

If their institutions are to be sustainable, the faculty, presidents, and boards must ask the following difficult questions within the context of their mission:

- What are the outcomes we expect of our students? How do these outcomes lead to student success? Are these the outcomes that will attract students, faculty members, and funding to our institution?

- Is our revenue model sustainable? How do demographic changes affect enrollment? What impact might the existence of our competitors—including for-profit and totally online providers—have on our institution? What are the implications of students increasingly tending to move from institution to institution?

- How will our institution respond to students, parents, elected officials, and others who call for stronger career outcomes, lower costs, lower debt levels, and more institutional accountability?

- To remain affordable and a good value to students, how can we become more productive and efficient? Should we reduce our expenses and by how much? How can we best use technology to reduce administrative costs and, perhaps, teaching costs through hybrid courses or curricula or other means? How can we manage faculty reductions?

- How do we build capacity within our board, administration, and faculty to boldly address needs for significant change? How can our institution foster faculty and administrative creativity, innovation, and entrepreneurship?

In effective organizations, such strategic questions are asked before the tactical questions. Board members, presidents, and faculty are often more comfortable with tactics, which are more controllable and concrete. But effective leaders today collaborate on developing strategies and building support for those strategies, often leaving the implementation of tactics to others.

A Shared Set of Metrics to Measure Success

Discussing the difficult issues associated with transformative change and developing mutually accepted strategies for achieving it are only the first steps. Effective systems of shared governance develop a series of agreed-upon metrics to measure success.

Too often the metrics for measuring success are input-focused because the inputs can be easily measured—student credentials, dollars spent per student, or percentile rankings of faculty salaries. Students, parents, and policymakers have made it clear that they are measuring institutions' performance according to the outputs. Students and parents demand high graduation rates, career development, and job placement. Policymakers demand a return on the public investment in higher education in the form of workforce development, access, and affordability.

While institutions typically have much more nuanced goals for student-learning outcomes than those related to graduates' ability to find jobs or pay off their loans, developing sensible output-oriented metrics is often difficult and subjective. Whether students are achieving the institution's goals for their learning outcomes is possible to measure, but the measurements are not as exact. They might involve student satisfaction, student retention, alumni satisfaction, and job placement and graduate-school acceptance rates, for example. Discussion with faculty of metrics to measure institutional and student success is likely to be vigorous and yet can lead to greater trust between the board and the faculty. (See Chapter 6 for more about the significance of trust and respect in shared governance.)

While boards are not sharing governance effectively when they get into the weeds of academic decisions, it is an appropriate board role to hold the faculty accountable for ensuring that students achieve desired learning outcomes. The board should ask the faculty to develop these outcomes and provide convincing rationales that explain to the board—and to the public more generally—why the outcomes are appropriate. Since the board holds responsibility for oversight of the institution's educational quality, it should be satisfied that the outcomes identified are sufficient to measure student growth and to attract students, faculty, and funds to sustain the college.

Effective Checks and Balances to Ensure that the Institution Remains Mission-Focused

When shared governance aligns priorities, it supports the institution making broad directional decisions, including identifying student-learning outcomes, strategic planning, program realignment, and hiring presidents and chief academic officers. But a system of shared governance also needs to address core operational decisions—including budget decisions and student-life decisions, and academic decisions such as programs of study and decisions on faculty hiring, tenure, and promotion. A system of shared governance should incorporate a set of checks and balances for this type of decision making.

For example, although matters of faculty appointments, tenure, and promotion are primarily within the domain of faculty, the limited review by the president and board helps give the system integrity. And although curriculum is squarely within the domain of the faculty, shared governance and institutional quality are enhanced when the board asks tough questions and when the president reminds the faculty of the fiscal constraints associated with program offerings.

Similarly, though finances are within the domain of the board and the administration, it can be valuable to have faculty members discuss whether budgets sufficiently support student learning, advising, faculty and student research, and community service. At its best, the budget process must be transparent. Difficult questions (and even impertinent questions) from the faculty should be regarded as important contributions to the debate. These tough questions might lead to a desirable re-examination of the budget in a way that better serves the institution. (See also Chapter 6.)

Checks and balances are often informed by the "AGB Statement on Board Responsibility for Institutional Governance", the AAUP "Statement of Government of Colleges and Universities" (see Chapter 3), and by provisions written into the institution's policies, particularly faculty handbooks. While these provisions are not sufficient to align goals for directional decisions, they are necessary to efficiently and effectively allocate responsibility for the hundreds of day-to-day decisions institutions make, where the authority of the board, faculty, and president overlap.

CONCLUSION

The three traditional views of shared governance promote fragmentation, not engaged, participatory decision making. As they face growing pressures for significant change, universities and colleges should pursue a different model, one that better satisfies the imperatives for shared governance. A more constructive model is centered on a system to align faculty, board, and administration in common directions for decision making regarding institutional direction, supported by a system of checks and balances for non-directional decisions. Decisions will be higher quality and more effectively implemented under this approach. And because this process of alignment is forward-focused, decisions do not dwell on yesterday's issues. Instead, it creates shared responsibilities for institutional sustainability and excellence.

Chapter 3. Shared Governance:
Law and Policy

Faculty involvement in academic governance has much to recommend it as a matter of academic policy, but it finds no basis in the Constitution.—Supreme Court of the United States in *Minnesota State Board for Community Colleges v. Knight* (1984)

REQUIREMENTS IN STATE LAW SET THE BASELINE FOR HOW COLLEGES and universities are governed. Beyond that general baseline, state law leaves institutions a great deal of latitude to develop their own systems of governance. Because of this latitude, college and university charters and bylaws, accreditation agencies, higher-education organizations, and collective-bargaining agreements often fill in the gaps on how colleges and universities should be governed, including defining the role of shared governance.

For private institutions, state laws governing nonprofit corporations apply to colleges and universities, as well as to churches, hospitals, social-service agencies, and cultural institutions. State nonprofit corporation statutes are quite general and do not mention shared governance.

Public institutions of higher education are established by state statute or constitution and governed by their chartering documents and any rules and regulations promulgated by their states. While these rules and regulations may touch on shared governance, they are often so general as to provide little practical guidance.

STATE LAW AND SHARED GOVERNANCE

The Model Nonprofit Corporation Act, adopted by the majority of the states, provides that "all corporate powers must be exercised by or under the authority of the board of directors of the nonprofit corporation, and the activities and affairs of the corporation must be managed by or under the direction, and subject to the oversight, of its board of directors." Those states not formally adopting this act have all enacted legislation with similar language.

Shared Governance and Academic Freedom

Shared governance and academic freedom are closely linked. Academic freedom, a principle long recognized by the courts and firmly entrenched in higher education, provides faculty members with the freedom to express their views in the classroom and in their research and to serve without fear of reprisals from their institutions. Faculty members have the right to express their views even when they may be unpopular or go against the commonly held beliefs of others within the institution. The First Amendment provides these rights to public institutions. Most private institutions have adopted policies providing faculty with similar rights.

Whether academic freedom extends beyond the classroom and research to faculty members' right to publicly comment on and criticize their institution's policies and practices is less clear. The Supreme Court's 2006 *Garcetti v. Ceballos* decision muddied the waters by reserving judgment on the issue of whether the First Amendment protects faculty in these circumstances. Since then, lower-court decisions have split on whether the First Amendment shields faculty members against adverse action when they criticize their administrations. Nonetheless, many universities have adopted policies that prohibit retaliation against faculty critics. As a general rule, it is advisable for institutions not to sanction faculty members who are critical, because while their criticism of policies may cause discomfort for the board or administration, the criticism may contain information that might help improve institutional policies and practices.

Systems of shared governance must recognize the faculty's freedom and responsibility to develop academic programs, determine student-learning goals, and decide how those goals are assessed. But the rights of faculty members to determine overarching academic policies and programs at their institutions are not as absolute as their rights to express their views in the classroom. Faculties' traditional rights and obligations to develop academic programs are subject to the board's general duty of oversight under state law. For example, while the faculty may propose a new program, boards, with the advice of the administration, determine whether and at what level to fund the program.

Faculty rights to participate in determining administrative actions—such as budgets, facilities decisions, administrative structures, and administrative hires—are more constrained than their central role in academic policies. Here, academic freedom includes the right to be heard and the right to comment on, recommend, or criticize policies without fear of repercussion. But it does not extend to the right to veto key administrative determinations traditionally within the primary domain of the administration.

The language of the act is important. Boards are not actually required to manage the activities of the nonprofit corporation, but they are allowed to have the activities managed by someone else *under their direction.* The act specifically allows the board to delegate many of its responsibilities to committees.

In addition, boards almost always delegate day-to-day matters to the officers of the organization, subject to their continuing obligation to monitor the activity of those to whom they delegate. In the same vein, boards may also delegate certain decisions to the president, chief academic officer, and the faculty, such as control of academic programs, so long as the programs are still generally under their supervision. The Model Nonprofit Corporation Act cautions, however, that the delegation of authority to others "does not alone constitute compliance by a director with the standards of conduct."

In what has been dubbed the "business judgment rule," the Model Nonprofit Corporation Act requires directors to "act in good faith, and in a manner the directors reasonably believe to be in the best interests of the nonprofit corporation." This provides little practical guidance for directors. What is good faith? Is it subjective good faith, as in "I intended to govern well"? Or is it objective good faith, as in "I acted as a reasonable director would act"?

Fortunately, the Model Nonprofit Business Corporation Act is illuminated by cases decided by the courts in each of the 50 states. Although these cases have their own nuances, the thrust of most decisions is similar:

- **Board members must inform themselves adequately before making decisions.** They can rely on the expertise of others, but they must reasonably believe, after investigation, that those they are relying on have sufficient expertise and are reliable.

- **Board members must act in good faith, measured by a "reasonable director" standard.** It is not enough to have good intentions. Rather, board members must act as other reasonable board members in their positions would act.

- **Board members are responsible for the actions they delegate to others, and they must not abdicate their duty to supervise those to whom they delegate.** Board members, as part of their duty of supervision, must believe that the persons to whom they delegate authority are competent and reliable. Directors must also believe that those to whom they delegate authority can undertake that responsibility without conflict of interest.

- **Boards are responsible for evaluating the actions of those to whom they delegate responsibility.** Unexamined or uninformed acceptance of recommendations or turning a blind eye to the actions of others is unacceptable. Instead, board members must act as reasonable board members would in using their own judgment, gathering sufficient information to know whether the decisions made under their direction or delegation are reasonably within the best interest of the organization.

- **Board members must be timely in their attention and ongoing oversight.** When facts arise that should alert a reasonable director to a problem, the board must be reasonably attentive and timely in addressing the problem.

What does this all mean for shared governance? Shared governance is functional when the board delegates or shares its authority with others. Boards that share governance delegate powers through provisions in their governing documents or faculty handbooks (developed by the faculty and presented to the board for approval). Similarly, they can delegate through endorsement of standards of shared governance recommended by higher-education associations or collective-bargaining agreements or through consistently following ad hoc practices that defer to faculty on certain matters. And just as a board can delegate, absent a contract or other provision, it can take back what it delegates.

It is clear that without a board's delegation of authority, there is no legal right to shared governance. In the seminal United States Supreme Court case of *Minnesota State Board for Community Colleges v. Knight*, decided in 1984, Justice Sandra Day O'Connor speaking for the court found the following:

To be sure, there is a strong, if not universal or uniform, tradition of faculty participation in school governance, and there are numerous policy arguments to support such participation. But this Court has never recognized a constitutional right of faculty to participate in policymaking in academic institutions.... Even assuming that speech rights guaranteed by the First Amendment take on a special meaning in an academic setting, they do not require the government to allow teachers employed by it to participate in institutional policymaking.

HIGHER-EDUCATION ASSOCIATIONS AND SHARED GOVERNANCE

The Association of Governing Boards of Universities and Colleges, American Council on Education, and American Association of University Professors have each strongly endorsed the concept of shared governance. Although there may be differences over some details, they do agree that the faculty is central to developing and delivering the academic program and that the board has general oversight authority over the institution.

The "AGB Statement of Board Accountability," adopted by its board in 2007, provides that boards have a general "fiduciary responsibility to advance the institution's mission and to promote the institution's integrity and quality." Central to the institution's integrity and quality is the educational program. The AGB statement, consistent with state law, recognizes that the board "determines generally the types of academic programs the institution shall offer to students, and is ultimately accountable for the quality of the learning experience." But it also recognizes that faculty and academic administrators "shape the manner in which subjects are taught and learning experiences framed, identify who shall teach these programs, and develop approaches to assess the outcomes of student learning."

AGB further clarified its view of boards' responsibility for the academic programs in its "Statement on Board Responsibility for the Oversight of Educational Quality," released in 2011. This document clearly endorses shared governance, while also making it clear that boards must hold faculties and administrations accountable for educational quality.

The AGB statement fills important gaps in state law about how boards can best discharge their fiduciary responsibilities (see Exhibit 4). And the AGB documents cited provide practical guidance about questions board members should ask concerning the academic program in order to discharge their responsibilities of oversight:

> While academic administrators and faculty members are responsible for setting learning goals, developing and offering academic courses and programs, and assessing the quality of those courses and programs, boards cannot delegate away their governance responsibilities for educational quality. The board's responsibility in this area is to recognize and support faculty leaders in continuously improving academic programs and

---

Exhibit 4. AGB's Principles of Board Oversight of Academic Programs

The governing board should commit to developing its capacity for ensuring educational quality.

The board should ensure that policies and practices are in place and effectively implemented to promote education quality.

The board should charge the president and chief academic officer with ensuring that student learning is assessed, data about outcomes are gathered, results are shared with the board and all involved constituents, and deficiencies and improvement are tracked.

The board is responsible for approving and monitoring the financial resources committed to support a high-quality educational experience.

The board should develop an understanding of the institution's academic program—undergraduate, graduate, and professional programs.

The board should ensure that the institution's programs and resources are focused on the total educational experience, not just traditional classroom activities.

The board should develop a working knowledge of accreditation: what it is, what process it employs, and what role the board plays in that process.

Source: "AGB Statement on Board Responsibility for the Oversight of Educational Quality," (AGB, 2011).

---

outcomes, while also holding them—through institutional administrators—accountable for educational quality.

The 1966 AAUP *Statement of Government of Colleges and Universities* is the most commonly discussed statement regarding shared governance as a defined set of rules of engagement. It remains the standard at many colleges and universities, with its principles often incorporated into faculty handbooks, state university regulations, union contracts, and policy statements. The statement says that the faculty should have primary responsibility for making recommendations in the following areas, which cover the academic waterfront:

- Course requirements
- Degree requirements
- Faculty status, including hiring and tenure decisions
- Appointment of academic department chairs
- Selection and organization of faculty representative structures

The statement recognizes that certain faculty decisions are subject to review, however. On matters of faculty appointments, tenure, and promotion, it recognizes limited authority of the president and board to review faculty decisions.

Though it advocates for broad delegation of authority, the statement recognizes that the board has primary responsibility for the following:

- Ensuring fidelity to mission
- Managing the endowment
- Managing the finances of the college—both for operating expenses and capital needs
- Setting general personnel policies that govern all employees

The statement recognizes that the following responsibilities are primarily the domain of the president:

- Planning for the institution
- Maintaining instructional resources and developing new resources
- Managing non-academic activities
- Serving as chief spokesperson

The AAUP statement thus recognizes that the faculty, the board, and the administration have different areas of primary responsibility and that those areas of responsibility overlap. It also recognizes that "the variety and complexity of the tasks performed by institutions of higher education produce an inescapable interdependence among governing board, administration, faculty, students, and others. The relationship calls for adequate communication among these components, and full opportunity for appropriate joint planning and effort."

While the AAUP statement is helpful as a starting point for how the board might delegate certain tasks pertaining to academic programs to the chief academic officer and the faculty, it implicitly treats this delegation as setting boundaries (and creates a sense of territoriality within those boundaries) when various constituencies differ. The statement does not sufficiently emphasize the board's ultimate responsibility, even when it delegates some responsibility to others, for ensuring that policies (developed by the administration and/or the faculty) promote education quality. Nor, in today's world of transformative change, does it foster effective and efficient practices that are necessary for aligning the board, faculty, and administration around priorities that will propel the institution forward.

ACCREDITATION AND SHARED GOVERNANCE

Accrediting agencies often mandate some level of shared governance as a condition of accreditation. For example, the Middle States Commission on Higher Education states the following:

> The Commission on Higher Education expects a climate of shared collegial governance in which all constituencies (such as faculty, administration, staff, students, and governing board members, as determined by each institution) involved in carrying out the institution's mission and goals participate in the governance function in a manner appropriate to that institution.

Accreditation standards vary from one regional accrediting commission to another. Most commissions state their general support for shared governance but do not prescribe specific practices for implementing it. As a general rule, most accreditation commissions touch on the following general standards in their accreditation regulations:

- Institutions should provide some level of shared governance.
- Open communication among all constituencies is important.
- The faculty has primary responsibility for the content and structure of academic programs, as well as faculty personnel matters.
- The faculty should have a role in institutional planning.
- Governance policies and procedures should clearly specify which groups have what responsibilities.

In addition, specialized accreditation commissions often mandate similar participation by faculty in academic decisions and in academic planning.

GOVERNING DOCUMENTS AND SHARED GOVERNANCE

Because principles of shared governance are longstanding traditions in higher education, they are often firmly ensconced in the policy documents of each college or university. These organizational documents usually enumerate the powers of the faculty, the board, and the president. For multi-university systems, there are often system-wide policies concerning governance, provided by state regulations, the board of regents, system-wide academic senates or assemblies, or the systems' chancellor. (See also "System-Wide Shared Governance" in Chapter 2.)

Although state law varies, faculty handbooks often are considered part of a contract between faculty and the institution and are enforceable as such. The AAUP has prepared an excellent analysis of state laws concerning the legal enforceability of provisions in faculty handbooks in its publication, *Faculty Handbooks as Enforceable Contracts: A State Guide*. Increasingly, colleges and universities explicitly state that faculty handbooks are intended to be statements of practice, not contracts, and that the board can amend them at any time. Boards also often stipulate that they must approve any amendments to the faculty handbook made by the faculty.

As part of a shared governance system, faculties and boards must become familiar with the contents of faculty handbooks and whether, under state law and/or the provisions of the handbook, the provisions may be enforceable as contracts. Faculty members tend to view them as fundamental contractual provisions, and when boards do not follow them, faculty may cry foul and believe that boards are riding roughshod over shared governance.

SHARED GOVERNANCE RIGHTS IN COLLECTIVE-BARGAINING ENVIRONMENTS

Institutions with faculty collective-bargaining agreements may find elements of shared governance specified as part of the collective-bargaining agreement. On other campuses, union agreements may focus on wages and benefits, rather than broader governance concerns. When shared-governance rights are included in collective-bargaining agreements, these rights are legally enforceable by the courts. In most cases, they are also subject to quicker enforcement by arbitration procedures.

Collective-bargaining agreements usually define the right of the faculty senate to participate in governance, including faculty involvement in appointments, reappointments, and tenure and promotion. Bargaining agreements often establish rights in cases of retrenchment and reductions in the number of faculty positions. These agreements might also provide faculty rights to sit on search committees for presidents and chief academic officers, as well as participation on other institution-wide committees, such as budget committees. Collective-bargaining agreements almost always state that faculty members and their leaders have rights to timely information on the institution's policies and finances.

Due to the great variation in whether or how collective-bargaining agreements deal with issues of shared governance—and also because the Supreme Court has held that faculty members at private institutions cannot unionize—a detailed discussion of issues of collective bargaining and shared governance is beyond the scope of this book. For readers at institutions where faculty collective-bargaining agreements are in force, helpful discussion of the treatment of shared governance may be found in such resources as Kenneth P. Mortimer's chapter "The Board's Role in Collective Bargaining" (in *Governing Public Colleges and Universities* by Richard T. Ingram, Jossey-Bass 1993) and William L. Perry's "Observations on Entering a Collective Bargaining Environment" (*Journal of Collective Bargaining in Higher Education,* Vol. 2, December 2010).

CONCLUSION

As this chapter demonstrates, state law provides underlying principles for shared governance. It provides that governance can be shared, but sharing governance does not relieve boards of their general obligations to engage in careful supervision of their institutions. State law does not generally provide detailed guidance about how governance might be practically shared, however. Accordingly, boards have had to look elsewhere to fill the gap. Higher-education associations provide valuable practical guides on how to share governance. In addition, faculty handbooks, collective-bargaining agreements, accreditation rules, and ad hoc practices typically define more specifically how governance is shared.

Chapter 4. Overcoming Barriers to Effective Shared Governance

There are no constraints on the human mind, no walls around the human spirit, no barriers to our progress except those we ourselves erect.—President Ronald Reagan, "Address Before a Joint Session of the Congress on the State of the Union" (February 6, 1985)

SHARED GOVERNANCE IS MOST LIKELY TO BE EFFECTIVE WHEN BOARD members, administrators and faculty members recognize three types of barriers and address them effectively: attitudinal barriers, structural barriers, and behavioral barriers. Fortunately, when these barriers are understood and appreciated, it is possible to deal with the challenges they present.

ATTITUDINAL BARRIERS

Early in my presidency, I had a memorable conversation with our then-board chair, Brenda Barnes, who had been CEO of PepsiCo North America. I told her that I believed that serving as a college president was quite different from serving as a CEO of a Fortune 500 corporation. I explained that implementing policies was much more difficult at colleges and universities than at business corporations, particularly because moving tenured faculty members forward was sometimes difficult. She retorted that members of her team did not have "legal" tenure but that they had "effective" tenure. As president of a corporation in a highly competitive business, she said her vice presidents were effectively tenured because they were so instrumental to the success of the business. She needed to build trust and goodwill with her key employees, just as presidents and boards need to with the faculty. When trust is built and nurtured, it can ease the process of implementing decisions in a timely way.

An AGB study, on *Faculty, Governing Boards, and Institutional Governance,* points to a lack of mutual understanding and respect as an obstacle to effective shared governance. If faculty members don't trust the administration, they will not invest their time in governance, particularly when they are more comfortable in the classroom and with their research. If the constituencies don't trust each other, they will not share ideas. The willingness to compromise also requires trust, because compromise often necessitates choosing to pursue a common agenda rather than a personal one.

Faculty members, administrators, and board members do have differing outlooks, primarily because they have different roles and vantage points at the institution. Often they do not know each other well and do not have the opportunity to understand the differences among their cultures and roles. As a result, they may revert to deeply ingrained popular myths about the other parties.

Among the myths that faculty members may hold about board members are the following:

1. They are "suits" who engage in drive-by management.
2. They seek prestige and bragging rights about their alma mater.
3. They are bean counters who want to run a college like a corporation, based on the bottom line.
4. They are motivated by nostalgia for the good old days, which they want to revive.

Yet when faculty members have the opportunity to spend time with board members, many quickly learn that board members' passion for their institutions, though expressed in different language, is as deep as their own.

Faculty members are not alone in myth making. Common board member myths about faculty that interfere with trust include the following:

1. Dealing with professors is like herding cats.
2. Faculty members like to talk about problems, but do not really want to make the hard decisions needed to solve them.
3. There is really only one way to work with the faculty: Find the path of least resistance and proceed accordingly.
4. Faculty members are professional contrarians, and the academy rewards them for it by giving them tenure.

Board members who get to know faculty members come to understand that it is tenured faculty, most of whom have made life-long commitments to the institution, who are the first to remind us of the core mission and values that sustain the institution's overall commitment to quality.

This is not to say that there are no differences in a typical institution between how faculty members think and how board members think. For example:

- Faculty members are prone to view accountability as being guaranteed the right to participate in the process of decision making, while board members define it as achieving results.
- Faculty members often lack the board's sense of urgency.
- Faculty members tend to seek excellence within departmental boundaries, while board members take a broader view of the institution.
- Faculty members tend to view decision making as a collegial process involving thorough vetting of all positions, while board members view it more hierarchically.

These differences can be viewed as impediments to shared governance and integral leadership. A better way to view these differences, though, is as creative tensions that can help guard against the precipitous decisions sometimes found in hierarchical governance. When the parties can come to respect the perspectives and vantage points of other stakeholders, leaders may be able to engage in better and more deliberate communication and, ultimately, higher-quality decision making.

STRUCTURAL BARRIERS

There are four primary structural barriers to effective shared governance:

- Faculties too fragmented to govern themselves
- Weak administrations too decentralized to speak with one voice
- Boards that are divided and don't speak with one voice
- Governing documents that are incomplete, outdated, not understood, or not followed

Ineffective Faculty Governance

Effective faculty governance depends on participation by the faculty, and the composition of the faculty has changed dramatically over the years. One of the critical challenges to faculty participation is the rise in the proportion of adjunct faculty and other non-tenure-track faculty. In fact, adjuncts now make up the majority of faculty at America's colleges and universities, a dramatic change from 25 years ago (see Exhibit 5). Yet they are often not involved in formal faculty governance structures and, hence, are not effectively involved in shared governance. Many institutions do not provide meaningful representation of adjunct faculty in faculty senates, even when they teach the largest number of courses and even though the AAUP recommends that "no faculty member should be excluded from participation in governance because of the appointment conditions over which most have little control."

Even when adjunct faculty members are permitted, and even encouraged, to participate in governance, many do not. Many are working multiple part-time positions and simply do not have time to engage at any of their institutions. To the extent they and/or their institutions view them as not central to the academic program, they are not likely to invest the time needed to continuously improve academic programs. The anomalous result is that, at some institutions, those doing most of the teaching have the least investment in the institutions' teaching missions.

Involving more adjunct faculty members in governance is not always easy to achieve. Because the faculty has primary responsibility for determining how it organizes itself, including which categories of faculty participate in governance and on faculty senates, boards and presidents cannot, by fiat, mandate greater inclusion of adjunct faculty. But they can consistently urge faculty leaders and deliberative bodies to do so.

Many institutions are also witnessing the fragile nature of effective faculty governance. Quorums at full faculty meetings and full faculty senate meetings are harder to achieve. Often the colleagues that the faculty would like to elect for leadership positions bow out of contention because of personal and professional priorities that they see as more pressing (and perhaps less stressful).

Exhibit 5. Instructional Staff Employment Status: 1975, 2009

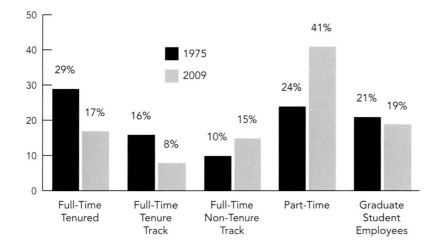

Source: Snyder T.D. and S.A. Dillow. *Digest of Education Statistics 2011 (NCES 2012-001)*. Washington, D.C.: National Center for Education Statistics, Institute of Education Sciences, U.S. Department of Education, 2012.

And, increasingly, faculty members tend to see themselves as primarily part of a department and an academic discipline, not as much a part of their college or university. This is often the case with adjunct or part-time faculty.

Faculties that are dysfunctional in their own operations will have a difficult time sharing governance. Effective faculty governance of the academic program includes some centralization, so that boards wanting to work with the faculty can identify those who have a legitimate claim as faculty leaders.

In a recent AGB survey of presidents, board chairs, and chief academic officers, 90 percent stated their colleges or universities had an institution-wide faculty governing body and 92 percent agreed the influence of the faculty governing body was "important" or "very important" to their institutions (*Faculty, Governing Boards, and Institutional Governance,* AGB, 2009).

Faculty members are less satisfied with how institution-wide faculty governing bodies operate. In a national survey by William G. Tierney and James T. Minor, 53 percent reported "a low level of interest in Senate activities," 43 percent stated that "involvement in the Senate was not highly valued," and 31 percent agreed that the "goals of the Senate were not clearly defined" (*Challenges for Governance: A National Report,* 2003).

Often when the faculty senate is weak, academic departments are strong. And when the locus of faculty decision making is at the individual departmental level, overall institutional academic planning is difficult, particularly when academic departments have differing views on college-wide issues.

Boards and administrations that encourage and foster strong and more centralized systems of faculty governance are more likely to enjoy effective shared governance. Board members can help strengthen faculty senates and other organs of faculty governance through such means as publicly affirming their importance, consistently involving faculty leaders in discussions at board meetings on faculty issues, and including faculty leaders in campus leadership training programs.

Ineffective Administrative Structures

College and university administrations can likewise be too decentralized. If decision making is too far dispersed throughout a university to colleges and schools or within a college to departments, the faculty and even administrators

Faculty Senates and Assemblies

Most faculties organize themselves into some type of governing body—such as faculty senate or university assembly—to serve as a forum for addressing institution-wide issues, shaping policies, and speaking with a single representative voice to the president, other administrators, and the board. The faculty governing body is often an elected group and is designed to be broadly representative of the faculty (and sometimes staff and students). Depending on the issue, situation, and institution, its role may be to influence policy, advise the administration on policy, or make policy—in line with the role of faculty in shared governance.

Because of the wide range of expectations for faculty work and institutional traditions, there is no single best structure for a faculty governing body. On many campuses, the faculty senate is representative; at others it may be a body of the whole. On some campuses, it includes only full-time, tenured faculty; increasingly, however, it includes non-tenured and adjunct faculty. Some campus governance bodies also include students, staff, and senior administrators. The most effective faculty senates cycle leaders through from across the campus (faculty from different disciplines, years of service, and perspectives).

Source: *What Board Members Need to Know About Faculty* by Cathy A. Trower and R. Barbara Gitenstein (AGB Press, 2013).

can become frustrated with not knowing whom to deal with and who can make decisions. For example, if professional schools have significant autonomy from other schools within a university, it is difficult for a central administration to speak for the entire institution, which makes sharing governance with the faculty all the more difficult.

Also critical to an effective administration are healthy relationships between the president and key administrative cabinet members, particularly the chief academic officer. Shared governance functions best when the chief academic officer and the president agree on general approaches to academic issues. If the president and chief academic officer are divided, faculty members may play one against the other. The chief academic officer is usually the most important single person in facilitating shared governance at the day-to-day level. Indeed, making sure that the chief academic officer and faculty leaders interpret the faculty handbook similarly can head off some tensions over issues such as tenure and promotion. When the chief academic officer does not have the confidence of the faculty, it is nearly impossible to bring the faculty to the table.

Presidents and boards must be intentional in supporting strong chief academic officers. Faculty members need to see that their chief academic officer has legitimacy with their governing body. To demonstrate this legitimacy, presidents and boards should encourage chief academic officers to play a central role in board discussions of academic issues. Boards would be well advised to build strong academic affairs committees with actively involved board members, a pivotal role for the chief academic officer, and a strategic focus on educational quality and outcomes.

Similarly, if the chief academic officer and chief financial officer do not have a good working relationship, effective shared governance is more difficult. Board members often have a closer relationship with the chief financial officer than with the chief academic officer because they are more comfortable with financial matters than with the sometimes mystifying academic world. If these two important leaders are not on the same page, board and faculty members may play them against each other, which will undermine shared governance.

Board members can ask the president about the relationship between the institution's chief academic officer and its chief financial officer, and, if there are issues, the board should encourage the president to have candid conversations with the two and set clear expectations that they work together. Board members also can help by recognizing the difficult role of the chief academic officer and reminding the chief financial officer that while balanced budgets are a priority, the true bottom line of any college or university is not operating surpluses but achievement of student-learning outcomes.

Ineffective Board Structures or Leadership

Effective shared governance also requires effective board leadership. The same elements that can make faculty governance ineffective can make board governance ineffective—weak and indecisive leadership, deep divisions and factions, lack of collegial debate, or poor structures. And, although unusual, boards can be too centralized. If a full board is committed to shared governance, but the real decisions are made by an executive committee, finance committee, or academic affairs committee, shared governance is likely to be circumvented. Thus, effective shared governance requires an effective board chair. Because sharing governance might not come naturally to all board members, board chairs must be vocal and consistent advocates of shared governance, even when it may be cumbersome or frustrating.

The following attributes of boards help facilitate effective shared governance by building respect from the faculty:

- Boards that are well informed about academic matters are best able to engage in important conversations with faculty members about the academic program, effectively discharging their duty of oversight.
- Boards that understand and respect the importance of academic freedom will have the most productive relationships with the faculty.

- Boards that support the president, but hold the president accountable, will empower the president and gain credibility with the faculty.
- Boards that appropriately focus on strategic issues, not day-to-day issues, will best engage faculty members in the high-level, overarching conversations necessary to respond to changing circumstances.

When boards function effectively, faculty leaders will notice it. When boards are dysfunctional, faculty leaders will be less willing to engage in the sustained and hard work of shared governance.

Incomplete, Outdated, Misunderstood, or Ignored Governing Documents

It is difficult to share governance if practices within the institution are different from what the bylaws, faculty handbook, and other governing documents actually mandate. Revelations of such discrepancies can slow or sabotage decision making. The board's governance committee has responsibility for making sure appropriate policies exist, that they are up to date, and that they are consistent with actual practice. Chief academic officers and the institution's legal counsel should review these policies periodically. Boards and faculty often need to work together to improve imprecise or incomplete governing documents.

Worse than outdated policies are policies that are ignored by administrators. This happens quite often, as existing policies typically are voluminous, sometimes are not well organized, and frequently contain ambiguous language. Faculty members may use failure to follow policies as "Exhibit A" in arguing that the administration is not truly committed to shared governance.

"Governing documents should state who has the authority for specific decisions—that is, to which persons or bodies authority has been delegated and whether that which has been delegated is subject to board review." ("AGB Statement on Board Responsibility for Institutional Governance," 2010)

BEHAVIORAL BARRIERS

Even when institutions have proper structures in place to support shared governance, certain behaviors risk destroying the trust necessary for effective governance.

Presidential Divide-and-Conquer Philosophy

An all-too-common philosophy of presidents is to divide and conquer. Perhaps even playing on the myths discussed in this chapter, they may lead board members to believe that they really cannot trust the faculty to participate in meaningful shared governance. They may even position themselves as key to protecting the college from the naïve idealism and self-interest of the faculty. These same presidents will tell faculty members that they will protect them from the excesses of the board, playing on the idea that board members engage in drive-by management and do not really understand higher education. This strategy can be effective in the short-run, because it consolidates presidential power. But faculty members and board members inevitably talk with each other. And when they do, the president's behavior is revealed and his or her credibility is severely damaged.

Lack of Respect for the Faculty Leaders in Academic Matters

Board members—and the president—must be willing and able to show appropriate respect for faculty stewardship of the educational program and the centrality of the faculty in making academic decisions. They should do so because it is best for the institution. AGB's "Statement on Board Responsibility for the Oversight of Educational Quality" recognizes that boards must appropriately monitor these programs and assess outcomes but must allow faculty members the responsibility for "setting learning goals, developing and offering academic courses and programs, and assessing the quality of those courses and programs."

When board members intrude into areas traditionally reserved for the faculty, faculty members often react quickly and harshly. They appropriately view these board members as not respecting the faculty and not understanding the academic culture. Of course, board members can unwittingly cross the line into faculty territory. If they have ideas for program enhancements or academic improvements, they should tread gently. Suggestions can be made, but only as suggestions for consideration, while acknowledging the central role of faculty in curricular matters. Too often faculty members view board suggestions as mandates.

It is natural for boards, on occasion, to become frustrated with the faculty. Yet it is far better to make concerted efforts to build bridges with the faculty members than to let frustration about the faculty burn bridges with faculty leaders. Developing and maintaining trust between the board and the faculty, though hard work, will redound to the benefit of the institution and its students.

Overcoming Extreme Behaviors Undermining Shared Governance

It is unfortunately true that some participants in the shared governance process may seek to actively undermine the process, since sharing governance tends to level the playing field and may take away power from some parties or individuals. In other cases, for a variety of reasons, trust may have broken down to the extent that shared governance seems almost impossible. Thus it is useful to pinpoint some of the extreme behaviors and some strategies for getting governance back on track.

Troublesome actors include the following:

- Faculty members, administrators, or board members who have been given a "grumbler's veto" because the institution's leaders have allowed their complaining to derail progress even though these individuals have not been able to build consensus for their viewpoint.
- Presidents who allow select faculty members to serve as an informal "kitchen cabinet" that exercises influence without working through established shared governance processes.

- A board member, president, or faculty member who considers himself or herself the "smartest person in the room" and thus may lack the skills to listen or collaborate.
- Anyone participating in governance who lacks civility, constantly finds fault with others, and/or engages in *ad hominem* attacks and spreads rumors.

Neither an iron fist nor a kid glove is the best strategy in such circumstances. It helps to realize that dissenters, in some cases, may have the seeds of good ideas but have insufficient information or temperament to develop them fully. For a president, the following techniques may be helpful:

- Affirmatively invite everyone to make his or her views known and encourage discussion of divergent views before decisions are made, even if those views are ultimately rejected.
- Talk individually to those undermining governance and see what might bring them into the process. Some just want to vent and will accept a personal invitation to participate. Others may back off when their disrespectful behavior is pointed out in a one-on-one conversation.
- Accept that some individuals simply do not have the patience or disposition to participate in shared governance.
- Speak out against incivility—and try to insist that discussions take place face-to-face, not via e-mail. Presidents, board chairs, and faculty leaders should state publicly that ideas and positions might be subject to critical debate but that attacks on motives or individuals are not appropriate.

In some circumstances trust is deeply broken. Most commonly, the faculty has lost trust in the president. In my study of more than a dozen cases over the past two years, the most common facts were the following::

- The board and president agreed to substantially quicken the pace of change to respond to changing circumstances, without meaningful involvement of faculty.

No-Confidence Votes

The number of votes of no-confidence in presidents of institutions has grown rapidly in recent years. Many cases have occurred at high-profile research universities. The increase corresponds with the number of colleges and universities making significant decisions about their direction and the increasing sense among faculty members that they have not participated in those decisions. Within a one-year period, the faculty voted no-confidence at four prominent universities. At New York University, the College, of Arts and Science narrowly passed a vote of no-confidence in its president. The issue was the president's and board's plan to pursue global development plans, as well as a planned expansion in Greenwich Village. Emory University's administration proposed closing a handful of programs, prompting a similar outcry by the faculty. Administrators at St. Louis University proposed reforming the tenure system, causing faculty uproar. And at University of Northern Iowa, faculty members voted no confidence in both the president and provost after they made controversial budget cuts. In each case, faculty leaders expressed concern that the institutional missions were evolving without adequate consultation and engagement of faculty leaders. The best practices found in Chapter 6 can help boards, faculties, and administrations develop common understanding of how to share governance in difficult decisions about institutional direction.

- The president disagreed with and overruled key faculty decisions, including those regarding recommendations of tenure or significant restructuring or closing of academic departments, whether or not the president's positions were ultimately justified.
- Faculty members complained of low morale and accused the president of being dismissive, disrespectful, aloof, or uninterested in shared decision making.
- Inadvertent and ill-advised comments by the president (unfortunately, often about gender and race) became symbols of something larger, such as concerns about the president's lack of sensitivity toward others.
- Faculty members took their disputes to students, media, and the blogosphere.
- The board quickly and publicly backed the president without inviting further dialog, causing faculty members to escalate their rhetoric.

In many cases, the president had exacerbated the situation, for example, by refusing to meet with faculty leaders, failing to follow the faculty handbook on major decisions, neglecting or alienating key cabinet members, or hiding behind board decisions rather than explaining the rationales.

When shared governance processes are broken and the faculty and administration are at odds, leaders should ask whether a "reset" is possible with the aggrieved constituency. Some of the principles and practices described in detail in Chapter 6 can help to repair damaged relationships, including some sort of *mea culpa* by presidents and board chairs acknowledging their role in the problem. In addition, a survey to examine the health of the shared-governance system, a shared-governance task force, and other specific actions to attempt to rebuild trust can help. But sometimes, a reset among the current board chair, president, and faculty leaders is not possible. The lines have been too deeply drawn, or perhaps the president or board chair simply does not respect shared governance and never will. In those cases, it is important for the full board to determine if a change in leadership is necessary.

CONCLUSION

For many institutions, developing an understanding and appreciation for the barriers is the first step to effective shared governance. As frustrating as they can be, with sustained effort, these barriers generally can be removed. But savvy boards will also understand that drawing on the inherent differences between the faculty culture and the board culture can create a much more effective marketplace of ideas and facilitate making better decisions. They also will intervene when inappropriate behaviors either threaten to or have led to serious breakdowns in shared governance.

Chapter 5. A Practical Guide to Shared Governance

Coming together is a beginning; keeping together is progress; working together is success.—Henry Ford

HOW GOVERNANCE IS EFFECTIVELY SHARED IN PRACTICE VARIES depending on the type of decision. For decisions concerning the mission, direction, and values of the institution, shared governance is best employed to help align the priorities and views of the faculty, administration, and board. At other times, for decisions that are within the primary domain of the faculty or the board, shared governance can best provide needed consultation to ensure that high-quality decisions are made and understood by all. This chapter explores how shared governance functions in the following common categories of institutional decisions:

- **Strategic planning.** Meaningful faculty engagement in strategic planning is the best way to ensure that the board, faculty, and administration are fully aligned on important directions. This alignment helps ensure that strategic objectives will be pursued more effectively.

- **Student-learning outcomes.** Perhaps the most important, and most challenging, role of boards is to oversee academic programs. AGB states that the board's role is oversight, and the faculty's role is to develop and implement. Alignment between the faculty and the board fosters sharing responsibility for a strong academic program.

- **Direction and mission of the institution.** Such decisions often involve hiring a president or a provost and closing or realigning programs for financial or enrollment reasons.

- **Decisions primarily in the domain of the faculty.** These decisions include faculty hiring, tenure, and promotion; allocation of academic budgets; and faculty-handbook issues, including discipline of faculty members. Boards, however, still have general supervision over these matters, although they usually defer to the faculty responsible for reviewing the decisions.

• Decisions primarily in the domain of the board and administration.
These decisions include financial, student life, and other administrative
decisions traditionally within the domain of the president. Shared
governance is more important in business decisions directly affecting
the academic program.

STRATEGIC PLANNING

The greatest benefit of effective shared governance, particularly in times
of transformative change, is the ability to align priorities and create a sense of
shared responsibility for the outcomes. And the greatest opportunity for doing
so is to involve the faculty deeply and meaningfully in strategic planning. While
most agree that the president of the institution is its chief planning officer, a
president is seldom effective without the engagement of the faculty.

When faculty members consider strategic plans to be "top-down,"
they are not invested in their implementation. On the other hand, boards
sometimes view plans developed primarily by faculty as focused unduly on
maintaining existing silos instead of strategically advancing the institution.
Sharing governance through the strategic-planning process can avoid both of
these problems. Here are five intentional and thoughtful strategies that can
help create a sense of shared responsibility for making the plans successful:

1. **Properly structure a process that encourages broad involvement of the
   faculty.** It is important to state clearly at the outset that the plan, although
   finally approved by the board, is going to be developed organically by the
   larger community for the board's consideration. Thus the plan becomes
   collectively owned and is not simply the board's or the president's plan.
   The more shared interaction, deliberation, and discussion of strategies
   and objectives, the more legitimacy the plan will have.

2. **Carefully develop ground rules for strategic planning that maximize the
   probability of creating alignment.** Clear and realistic ground rules for the
   strategic-planning process should respect the extra time the process will

demand from the parties engaged in it. It is common for participants to feel that their time was wasted when they did not understand how the strategic planning process would unfold, its time-tables, and their role within it.

3. **Engage in deliberate discussions assessing the institution's competitive position as the landscape of higher education shifts.** Doing so directs attention away from individual agendas and toward a more data-driven and analysis-driven view of the institution and its challenges. Such analysis is especially important because the various stakeholders involved may view the competitive position very differently.

4. **Intentionally focus the initial discussions on strategies rather than tactics.** Too much emphasis on tactics at the expense of strategies will lead to a disjointed, uninspired strategic plan. Tactics, without strategies, focus on fixing past problems, not on identifying future opportunities.

5. **When developing and implementing tactics, respect the traditional vehicles of governance.** The faculty through its normal channels is responsible for the final vetting, approval, and implementation of tactics related to the academic program. The board finance committee is responsible for creating and allocating budgets for initiatives. And the president's office is responsible for refining an administrative structure to support the initiatives.

STUDENT-LEARNING OUTCOMES

If there is any common cause most faculty and board members can rally around, it is the welfare, growth, and achievement of students. In the widely discussed *Academically Adrift: Limited Learning on College Campuses* (2010), Richard Arum and Josipa Roksa argue that America's colleges and universities are falling far short in ensuring strong student-learning outcomes. The Association of Governing Boards has called the question of "how do we know how well our students are learning?" a fundamental one that should be a priority for every board.

When the board shares this focus with faculty, it helps board members discharge what is arguably their most important duty: overseeing the academic program. In addition, creating opportunities for faculty members, trustees, and administrators to discuss desired levels of student achievement *and* institutional outcomes is a highly effective way to help each constituency align priorities.

Responsibility for identifying, measuring, and assessing student-learning outcomes lies primarily with the faculty. Similarly, faculties are responsible for developing and offering courses and programs that deliver the important learning outcomes the faculty identifies. But boards remain responsible for ensuring that outcomes are, in fact, identified and assessed. Likewise, boards should hold the president and the chief academic officer accountable for ensuring that any deficiencies in student learning are identified and addressed. Boards should also ensure that student-learning outcomes are sufficiently tied to institutional missions and overall institutional effectiveness.

> "While academic administrators and faculty members are responsible for setting learning goals, developing and offering academic courses and programs, and assessing the quality of those courses and programs, boards cannot delegate away their governance responsibilities for educational quality." AGB Statement on Board Responsibility for the Oversight of Education Quality (2011)

To discharge the board's responsibilities for monitoring student outcomes, the academic affairs committee can invite the chief academic officer and faculty leaders to discuss desired student-learning outcomes. This whole area is sometimes overwhelming for board members because it is outside their comfort zones, but they can fulfill their responsibilities by asking questions, such as the following, and insisting on sufficient answers:

- What process does the faculty use to identify student-learning outcomes and educational quality? Are the outcomes widely accepted by the faculty and by departments?
- How do key features of the curriculum support learning outcomes? As learning outcomes are refined, is the curriculum modified?

- How does the institution assess whether students master the identified outcomes? What percentage of the students achieves all or most of the goals? What is the institution doing to increase that percentage?

- How does the institution assure that the quality of departmental assessment is consistent from department to department?

- Do faculty members have the resources to support student learning and mastery of the outcomes?

- Where can the institution improve, and what are the plans for doing so? How can the board help?

- Have accreditation agencies made findings about how effectively the institution is assessing student outcomes? If so, how is the institution responding?

- How do students' learning outcomes coordinate with student outcomes in student life, residential life, and athletics?

The "AGB Statement on Board Responsibility for the Oversight of Education Quality" (2011) provides an even more detailed list of questions that board members may find useful.

Working with the faculty to develop measures of institutional effectiveness

One of the best ways for the board and faculty to keep a focus on the measurement of outcomes is to develop an institutional-effectiveness dashboard that focuses on outcomes rather than inputs. Developing such a dashboard can engage the entire community in defining objectives, goals, and directions for the institution.

Most college dashboards are input-oriented and heavily tilted toward financial considerations. Inputs typically measured by these dashboards fail to provide enough information about whether the institution and its students are achieving the outcomes desired. Key outcomes for the faculty and board to assess, along with expected levels of achievement, include the following:

- Student persistence, graduation, and attrition rates. Consider analyzing these rates by demographic classifications.

- Program-participation rates (e.g., international programs, internships, student research, volunteering, athletics)

- Learning outcomes as measured by the National Survey for Student Engagement, the Collegiate Learning Assessment, or other means

- Overall satisfaction rates of graduating students, including how well they believe the institution prepared them for rewarding professional and personal lives or for graduate school

- Median level of student debt by program, as well as default rates

- Job-placement rates, focusing on full-time jobs preferring or requiring a college degree, as well as starting salaries

- Graduate-school placement rates, including percentage of graduates getting into one of their top three choices

DECISIONS ABOUT THE DIRECTION AND MISSION OF THE INSTITUTION

Decisions about the direction of the institution include appointing presidents or provosts and realigning or closing programs.

Hiring chief officers

"The board has a central role in shaping the composition of the search committee, which should consist of trustees, faculty members, and other stakeholders. ...Those appointed to a search committee must be reflective— though not necessarily 'representative'—of the different parts of the institution. Each member of a search committee must adopt a perspective that seeks to advance the institution as a whole, rather than harboring a constituency agenda concerned only with advancing a special school or unit." AGB, *The Leadership Imperative*, 2006

Selection of the institution's president is the most important decision a board makes because the president sets in motion the future course of the institution. Board members are responsible for selecting the president but should do so only after wide engagement by the community. This is best achieved by appointing a search committee that includes faculty members whose views are reflective of the faculty as a whole. A well-constituted search committee should not only recommend candidates but also help outline what is expected of the individual selected.

The president is ultimately responsible for the selection of the chief academic officer and other members of the president's cabinet, but consultation with faculty and board leaders is helpful. Faculty members have valuable insights, such as identifying the sort of candidate that tends to "manage up" to please the president but behaves like a tyrant to the faculty and other administrators. When faculty leaders participate in the selection process, they are much more likely to support the new chief academic officer when the going gets a bit rough.

Difficult decisions about the direction of academic programs

> "In response to financial challenges, many colleges and universities have pared spending significantly. They have moved quickly from relatively easy trims around the periphery of budgets to much more substantive cuts of programs and people. The economic pressures that have forced such reductions will very likely continue." *Top 10 Strategic Issues for Boards 2013–2014* (AGB Press, 2013).

Perhaps the most difficult areas in which to share governance are proposals for program realignment; shifts to a greater online presence; significant mid-year budget reductions; and reorganization of how the institution structures its academic program, closure of programs, or, in the extreme case, closure of the institution. Since the recession of 2008, there have been many high-profile conflicts among presidents, boards, and faculties over these difficult decisions.

In its publication *Top 10 Strategic Issues for Boards 2013–2014,* AGB called on institutions to develop a deeper sophistication in dealing with questions involving changes in institutional direction in light of the many pressures for change facing higher education. Decisions to change directions are best decided with sound data, transparent communication, robust debate, and a system of shared governance that aligns the goals of faculty members, administrators, and board members.

Program elimination is likely to put more stress on shared governance than virtually any decision an institution makes because of the impact on faculty jobs, future students, and the perceived erosion of the mission. Discontinuing a program—when called for by the administration or endorsed by the faculty senate—can tear at the collegiality that has built up at the institution over decades. And faculty members in other programs naturally ask whether their own program is next. For struggling institutions, closing or curtailing programs might be essential to continued financial viability. Likewise, program closures are often central to institutional strategies and directions.

The role of the faculty in program closures, particularly when faculty appointments are discontinued, is addressed by most faculty handbooks. An AAUP statement, *Financial Exigency, Academic Governance, and Related Matters,* notes that "effective collaboration among the faculty, administration, and governing board during a financial crisis requires that the collaborators be able to draw on a reservoir of mutual trust that has been built up in better days." The statement urges each constituency to ensure that established procedures are followed.

Almost all would agree that in times of financial hardship, boards have the right, and some would say the responsibility, to close or curtail programs *and* terminate some faculty appointments if necessary. But best practice requires that these difficult decisions, like other difficult academic decisions, be made through systems of shared governance. Best practices for boards and administrators in making difficult decisions for financial reasons include the following:

- **Build, in good times, a reserve of goodwill and trust sufficient to sustain the process of shared governance during difficult times.** Goodwill is advanced when faculty members have meaningful input into budgets, a firm understanding of budget realities, and a shared understanding of how academic programs align with mission and are evaluated.

- **Provide full disclosure to faculty members about the financial circumstances of the programs in question.** If administrators are concerned about breaches of confidentiality by faculty leaders, administrators can seek the informal agreement of faculty leaders concerning confidentiality expectations, although these expectations admittedly are hard to enforce.

- **Invite affected faculty members or faculty leaders to participate meaningfully in the discussions.** Faculty members should be invited to review and weigh in on the financial reasons for the proposed decision and alternatives to it. Faculty members might have useful ideas about increasing income, increasing enrollment, or reducing expenses that could avoid closing programs or terminating faculty appointments.

- **Create a meaningful opportunity for faculty leaders, when they disagree with the administration, to communicate their views to the board,** either through an opportunity to speak at the appropriate board committee meetings or to provide the board with a written report explaining why they disagree with the administration's position. Doing so creates a safety valve against pent up frustrations that might interfere with the institution's ability to make future difficult decisions.

In a study of colleges and universities that made difficult decisions such as closing programs ("The Role of Shared Governance in Institutional Hard Decisions: Enabler or Antagonist?" published in *The Review of Higher Education* in 2000), Peter D. Eckel found that when there are significant opportunities for collaboration, institutions were able to advance several important objectives, including the following:

- Providing a platform from which the board and administration were able to persuade campus consistencies of the seriousness of problems.

- Effectively bringing divergent interest groups together to "accomplish a high stakes task."

- Providing important checks and balances against making potential errors.

Eckel observed that decisions by boards to reduce student/faculty ratios, to shift more positions away from the tenure track, and to reconfigure academic buildings were improved using the vehicles of shared governance. Joint discussions can help move the faculty from territoriality to open, honest, and robust conversations that have the potential to find the best route in a difficult set of circumstances.

DECISIONS PRIMARILY WITHIN THE DOMAIN OF THE FACULTY

Although faculty members often fear that the board will micromanage academic programs, reports of boards doing so are extremely rare. The greater practical danger is that boards will effectively ignore oversight of academic programs, either because they are unfamiliar with the curriculum or because they trust the faculty to look after the academics.

Oversight of the academic program

AGB and AAUP agree that academic matters are primarily within the domain of faculty but that the board has general oversight of all aspects of the institution. Notable in AGB's "Statement on Board Responsibility for the Oversight of Educational Quality" is a statement of what boards are *not* responsible for. Boards are not responsible for setting learning goals, creating academic courses and programs, and assessing the quality of curricula. But, as discussed above, especially in the section on student-learning outcomes, the board *is* responsible for holding the institution and faculty accountable for educational quality.

Tenure and promotion

Board members may sometimes find tenure and promotion of faculty members a vexing area in which to share governance with the faculty. The real danger at most institutions is not micromanagement of this process but rather that boards will rubber stamp faculty recommendations. As a general matter, the core of tenure and promotion matters is within the domain of the faculty, because board members simply lack the expertise to make judgments as to the quality of teaching and faculty research. But the board does have a role and a responsibility here, and the following recommendations can help boards or their academic affairs committees to fulfill them:

- Board members should familiarize themselves with tenure standards. Periodically, the board should ask whether the standards are sufficiently rigorous (or too rigorous), perhaps comparing the standards to those at peer institutions. Similarly, the board should monitor faculty tenure by demographic data, including gender, racial/ethnic classifications, and academic areas. If disparities are apparent, the board should ask whether the tenure standards are being uniformly applied or whether they are structured or used in ways that disadvantage certain groups.

- Because of the significant liability and potential for bad decisions if the institution's processes are not followed, board members periodically should ask the chief academic officer to describe how compliance with the processes is monitored.

- At some institutions, procedures provide for an appeal to the board by faculty candidates of adverse tenure and promotion recommendations by the administration. If the board hears these appeals, it would be well advised to limit its review to three questions: Did the institution follow its own process and procedures? Was the process free from bias? Did the failure to recommend tenure for the candidate reflect the facts and represent a decision made by reasonable faculty members? By limiting appeals to these narrow grounds, boards will discourage appeals every time a faculty member is disappointed by a decision, while at the same time maintaining a needed check against poor decision making. Appeals of tenure recommendations decisions are extremely time-consuming, even if delegated to a committee. And board members usually do not have the best backgrounds to make these decisions.

DECISIONS PRIMARILY WITHIN THE DOMAIN OF THE ADMINISTRATION AND BOARD

Budget

Although decisions about the budget and other financial aspects of the institution—such as the draw rate from the endowment, investment policy, and the go-ahead for capital projects—are primarily within the domain of the administration and board, these are critical decisions for the academic program.

Approving the budget is a core responsibility of the board, based on recommendations from the institution's president and chief financial officer. Budget decisions seem much more complex today than even a decade ago. Undergirding financial decisions is a host of strategic issues, including several associated with systems of shared governance where the faculty's input can be quite helpful:

- How does the budget support both annual needs of the academic program, and the institution's longer term strategic plan?
- Does the budget provide support to improve the institution's identified student-learning outcomes and other institutional outcomes?
- Does the institution have well-developed revenue models, tuition strategies, and financial-aid models that are likely to support projected revenues while enrolling students who are likely to be academically successful?
- Does the budget control expenses and reflect hard financial decisions that allow the institution to both maintain a strong academic program and remain sustainable?
- Does the budget support innovative responses to the growing pressures for change in higher education, even if it means discontinuing support for other areas of the institution?

Presidents should consider using an internal campus budget committee, typically made up of faculty leaders, administrators, and sometimes students, as an advisory committee to the president and chief financial officer. The committee's charge should state clearly that it is advisory to president and not a policy-making committee. It is best when this committee is convened early in the budgeting process, before proposed budgets are created by the administration for board consideration. Using budget advisory committees of this type yields several advantages to institutions. These committees add to the transparency of the budgeting process so that faculty leaders better understand budget complexities and the institution's financial limitations. They can give presidents, and ultimately boards, valuable ideas about how budgets can best support agreed-upon initiatives to strengthen institutions. And they offer faculty members who serve on them an opportunity to provide valuable endorsements of the budgets and its priorities, which adds to goodwill and trust between faculty and administration.

Student Life

At one time, faculty members had much more control than they do now over decisions about admissions, student life, and athletics—areas that are now considered primarily administrative, with staffs dealing with student affairs. While some of this was a necessity given time demands on faculty and the growing complexity of these topics, faculty members are often closer to students and the prevailing student cultures than are administrators. Research into student outcomes has found advantages in an integrated approach to student growth through both academics and student-life activities. Thus, it may be time to consider how responsibility for student growth could involve more collaboration between the faculty and student life professionals. For example, faculty members may be the first to witness classroom challenges facing international students due to language, cultural norms, and teaching methodology. When faculty members work with student life professionals, they can identify such problems earlier and help develop appropriate interventions.

Systems of shared governance can create alignment in many areas of student life through consideration of the following questions:

- How does the institution's student-life program advance the institution's mission, values, and strategic plan?
- What are the preferred goals for student-life departments?
- Are the outcomes for student life aligned with academic outcomes?
- How can student-life activities prepare students for success after graduation?
- Are codes of student conduct and other student policies consistent with the institution's desired student-learning outcomes?

Sometimes it is advisable to appoint a faculty representative with a special obligation to delve more deeply into certain matters and to represent the faculty in administrative discussions of student life issues. This concept is not often employed beyond intercollegiate athletics, but it could be in such areas as admissions, campus safety, residential life, Greek life, and community outreach. Another way to increase faculty engagement in student life is to appoint advisory committees, with faculty members, administrators, students, and perhaps a board member, to help the president and student-life professionals monitor and improve student-life programs.

> "Boards should be confident that the institution's chief executive, academic, and athletic leaders have set appropriate standards of accountability and benchmarks against which to evaluate the success of the intercollegiate athletic program. These standards and benchmarks should encompass such areas as finances, admissions, student-athlete welfare, academic advising, graduation rates, facilities, capital expenditures, and conflict-of-interest policies." ("AGB Statement on Board Responsibilities for Intercollegiate Athletics," 2007.)

Other Administrative Decisions

Beyond the obvious area of budget and related financial decisions, a host of other administrative decisions is important to the vitality of the academic program. These include decisions about placement of facilities, location of academic and administrative offices, information-technology decisions,

Student Discipline

Boards should hesitate before considering appeals from students about disciplinary decisions made by the faculty or administration, either regarding academic issues or behavioral issues related to student life. Those appeals should be heard elsewhere in the institution, usually within the office of the chief academic officer or the dean of students. Agreeing to hear these appeals is a recipe for distracting the board from more important strategic issues. Further, delving deeply into the often-complicated details in these matters is not a board responsibility. And, when the board hears such student appeals, it invites disgruntled students and their lawyers to increase the number of defendants in any ensuing lawsuit.

The board's responsibility with respect to student behavior is, first, to ask whether codes of student conduct are sufficient to serve to keep students safe from their own destructive conduct (e.g., substance abuse) and from the potential harmful conduct of other students (e.g., sexual harassment, assault, hazing). Second, boards, through legal counsel, should examine whether codes provide a modicum of due process for the students. (Higher levels of detail are often required at public institutions.) Third, the board should ensure that the institution takes due-process protections for students seriously and routinely follows its own procedures. Boards can help ensure that institutions follow their own policies by insisting on at least one level of appeal within the institution, an effective whistleblower policy, and a periodic review by legal counsel of how the policies are administered.

admissions and financial-aid policies, marketing plans, and security and safety policies. While there is no single formula for involving shared governance in these decisions, the following techniques can help ensure that the input of all constituencies is considered:

1. Special task forces made up of faculty members, board members, and administrators to consider issues of institutional direction. Special task forces can be used to create an action plan to address important issues. Such a task force might be charged with creating a diversity action plan, for example, or an environmental sustainability action plan. Other areas where a joint task force might be successful include reviewing campus-wide safety issues, gender issues, workforce development, and community relations. In addition to wide representation from faculty, board members, and administrators, such a task force should include a few students. Asking faculty and student leaders to appoint their members of the task force can increase its credibility. The charge to such a task force should clearly identify the scope of its authority. Usually it is merely advisory.

2. Designation of a faculty advisory committee to the president or provost. It is not uncommon for presidents or provosts to appoint faculty members to a general committee to provide advice on a wide range of matters and to get a sense of faculty concerns. Some presidents and provosts pick the members; other presidents ask the faculty to elect all or most of the members in order to give the advisory committees more credibility with the faculty as a whole. For institutions with collective bargaining agreements, care should be taken not to ask advisory committees to review matters within the exclusive domain of the collective bargaining unit (i.e., terms and conditions of employment).

While the advice received from an advisory committee can be quite helpful, creating these committees is not without significant risk. If not carefully managed, a president could use the committee to supplant the work of elected and well-established faculty committees that have, as a part of their duties, the responsibility to advise the president. One president convened an informal "kitchen cabinet" of personal friends in the faculty and administration, whose preferences tended to overshadow the elected faculty senate. Similarly, using these committees may tempt some presidents to shortcut the hard work of reaching out to a broader array of faculty and involving them in a more meaningful way in the shared governance of the institution.

CONCLUSION

Effectively sharing governance and responsibility requires the hard work of aligning the goals and aspirations of the board, faculty, and the administration. But when institutions commit to taking practical steps to achieve effective shared governance, they will find discussions can become more future-oriented.

Chapter 6. Best Practices in Shared Governance

We may have all come on different ships, but we're in the same boat now.—Martin Luther King, Jr.

There is no strict formula for making shared governance work. In fact, shared governance begins with a quality that cannot be measured: trust. Developing trust and respect between board members and the faculty is critical to shared governance because those elements can sustain the faculty and board when mutual discussions become difficult. Trust helps nurture an environment in which it is safe for all constituencies to push and challenge each other respectfully.

Institutions can develop trust and goodwill through both formal actions—including transparency, honest and consistent messages from leaders, and respectful treatment of faculty members—and more informal means—inviting board members to observe a faculty meeting and attend a reception afterward or engaging the faculty with board members in assisting career-development offices to identify potential career paths for students.

Building on a foundation of trust and respect, five fundamental yet multifaceted practices can help institutions build a system of effective shared governance. Large universities with a variety of schools and colleges operate differently from small liberal arts colleges. Public institutions have different governing structures than do private institutions. But these best practices apply to all types of universities and colleges. They help connect board members, faculty members, and administrators in developing a shared sense of responsibility for the success of their institutions. These practices, which draw in particular on the discussion in Chapters 4 and 5, will help institutions develop a shared governance system that aligns institutional priorities and supports collaborative leadership.

Retreat to Advance Shared Governance

A few years ago, I invited an equal number of faculty members and board members to our annual board retreat to talk about the future of the college. I learned a couple of valuable lessons. The first lesson was how much faculty members want to be involved with board members. Our board retreat was held in a Chicago hotel, about a three-hour drive from our campus. The weekend of the retreat happened to be the weekend of the worst snowstorm in several years. A higher percentage of faculty invitees than board members made their way through the awful weather to the meeting. They were determined to make good on their opportunity to share governance.

The second lesson I learned was that faculty and board members are sensitive to issues of respect and collegiality. Board members dressed down a bit to relate to the faculty, and faculty members wore jackets and ties to relate to board members. It was quite a sight to see faculty members dressed like board members and board members dressed like faculty. But it reinforced the respect each constituency accorded the other and how much each constituency wanted to build goodwill.

That evening, the after-dinner conversations in the hotel lounge were not divided into faculty members and board members, but rather into small groups made up of faculty members, board members, administrators, and various spouses. As a result, several board members were invited by faculty members to give guest lectures in their classes, which board members viewed as an honor and a highlight of their board service.

CONSISTENTLY AND PUBLICLY REMIND ALL CONSTITUENCIES ABOUT THE IMPORTANCE OF SHARED GOVERNANCE

Concepts of shared governance are new to many board members. Board leaders, presidents, and chief academic officers must educate board members about the various definitions of and barriers to this system of aligning priorities. Following are some proven ways to help in this endeavor:

1.1 The president and board chair should be visible and effective advocates of shared governance. In particular, the president of the college or university is the key link between the faculty and the board, both of whom look to the president to help them understand how to work effectively with the

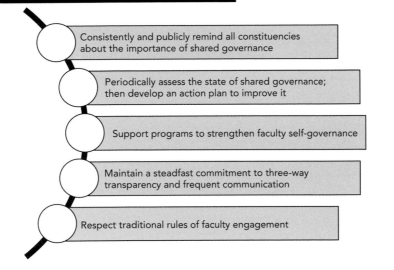

Exhibit 6: Shared Governance Best Practices

- Consistently and publicly remind all constituencies about the importance of shared governance
- Periodically assess the state of shared governance; then develop an action plan to improve it
- Support programs to strengthen faculty self-governance
- Maintain a steadfast commitment to three-way transparency and frequent communication
- Respect traditional rules of faculty engagement

other. The president must be able to explain the benefits of shared governance in terms embraced by all and be consistent in all messages to both the faculty and the board. Occasionally the president must slow important decisions until the shared-governance process has had a chance to work.

A good practice for presidents is to deliver the same state-of-the-college address to the faculty and staff that was delivered to the board, within a week of the board meeting. They often share these annual goals with the faculty first, as a gesture of goodwill and to receive their input. For complete transparency, many presidents also share the goals with the student-government association or student-advisory council to seek student input on the matters soon to be addressed by the board.

The board chair, chair of the academic affairs committee, and other board leaders must also demonstrate their commitment to shared governance and, by their actions, should make sure shared governance is valued and respected, even when it means decision making takes more time. Faculty will notice if shared governance processes are ignored.

1.2 Shared governance should be a central topic at board retreats and meetings. With the board chair as facilitator, the board can discuss the perspectives on shared governance outlined in Chapter 2. It is helpful to give the chief academic officer a central role, because he or she typically serves as a bridge between the faculty and the administration. Asking faculty leaders to participate in the discussion helps build trust with the faculty and helps board members understand how faculty might value shared governance differently.

If there has been tension among the faculty, board, and administration about leadership issues, it is sometimes helpful for the board to bring in a knowledgeable outside facilitator to lead the discussion. Doing so brings a level of neutral expertise to the table to help move the discussion forward.

1.3 Boards or board committees should consider including at least one member with experience as a faculty member to help explain faculty concerns and ways of operation to board members, who typically come from non-academic backgrounds. Usually that member is someone from outside of the institution, perhaps an alumnus who went on to a distinguished academic career somewhere else.

According to a 2010 AGB survey, at about a quarter of institutions, a current faculty member serves as a board member. AGB does not recommend that a current faculty member have voting rights on a board because of the potential for conflicts of interest, although some institutions do make this work. Instead, having faculty members participate in committees and make presentations at board meetings can help board members understand faculty perspectives.

PERIODICALLY ASSESS THE STATE OF SHARED GOVERNANCE AT THE INSTITUTION; THEN DEVELOP AN ACTION PLAN TO IMPROVE IT

An assessment of attitudes toward, and views of the effectiveness of, shared governance can help measure whether faculty members, administrators, and board members agree on how to define shared governance and how well each constituency believes the principles of shared governance are being honored.

A comprehensive assessment will give leaders on all sides a starting point from which to develop strategies to better align priorities and responsibilities.

Any assessment of shared governance is likely to reveal deep differences about the definition. A 2003 national survey, by William G. Tierney and James Minor, of academic vice presidents, faculty senate chairs, and faculty members found deep disagreement just among those parties. Nearly half defined shared governance as "fully collaborative decision making," meaning that the faculty and the administration should make decisions jointly and by consensus. About a quarter defined shared governance as consultative, with the faculty's voice being sought but with the authority to make decisions remaining with the administration and the board. The final quarter defined shared governance as distributive, meaning that decision making should be divided up by discrete areas, with faculty having authority in some areas and the board in others.

Methods for facilitating an assessment of perspectives on shared governance include the following:

2.1. Conduct a shared-governance survey of faculty, administrators, and board members. A sample survey is found in the Appendix. Board, administration, and faculty leaders can tailor it to reflect the structure, culture, and concerns of their institutions. Getting all parties to agree to the survey instrument is often the first step in reaching agreement on the larger issues associated with shared governance.

Board members and administrators need to thicken their skins before conducting surveys of faculty. In the Tierney and Minor survey, one-third of faculty respondents believed the level of communication among governing groups is inadequate. It is true that honest discussions of shared governance are not easy. Yet, when faculty, administrators, and boards discuss differing definitions and assessments of the current state of governance, each moves a bit closer to the others' positions.

2.2 Appoint a shared-governance task force. Shared-governance task forces provide an excellent forum for board members, faculty members, and administrators to discuss developing an action plan for how to improve shared governance. (See Exhibit 7 for a model of a charge to a task force.) Such a task force should have broad representation from the administration and current board and faculty leaders, ideally in equal numbers. Elected faculty leaders (e.g., officers of faculty senates or chairs of key committees) are likely to have a broader view of the institution.

To demonstrate the importance of the task force, the board chair (or vice chair) and chair of the board's academic affairs committee should serve. Some presidents choose not to serve, for fear that their presence might chill candid discussion. Instead, the chief academic officer could represent the president's office. Other good representatives include the vice president for student life and the chief enrollment officer.

SUPPORT PROGRAMS TO STRENGTHEN FACULTY SELF-GOVERNANCE

> "I would start by having faculty relearn the importance of collective actions—to talk less about shared governance, which too often has become a rhetorical sword to wield against an aggrandizing administration, and to talk instead about sharing responsibility for the work to be done together."—Robert Zemsky (*Checklist for Change: Making American Higher Education a Sustainable Enterprise,* 2013)

As explained in Chapter 4, if the faculty cannot govern itself effectively, it will not be able to share meaningfully in governance of the institution. A strong faculty, even a strong-willed faculty, is not inconsistent with shared governance. A faculty that can take strong, and sometimes bold, collective action is a necessary component of a shared commitment to moving the institution forward. Several practical and easy-to-take steps, however, may help strengthen faculty self-governance.

Exhibit 7. Sample Charge to a Shared Governance Committee

1. Prepare a summary of the results of the shared governance survey and an analysis of what is working well and what could work better.

2. Assess the adequacy of communication among various constituencies, the level of trust and understanding, and the degree of satisfaction with how governance is shared.

3. Assess whether the current mechanisms of shared governance (e.g., those found in charter documents, bylaws, collective-bargaining agreements, and/or the faculty handbook) are understood, followed, and respected.

4. If the provisions of the handbook are not being followed, recommend whether the provisions should be amended or whether greater efforts should be made to follow them.

5. Assess the strength of faculty governance of the academic program and whether the faculty-governance structure aids meaningful shared governance. Assess whether the board is familiar with the educational program and has asked questions about whether students are achieving desired learning outcomes.

6. Identify benchmarks of good shared governance.

7. Make three to five recommendations to be implemented within the next year to advance shared governance to close the gap between where the institution is and where it should be.

3.1 Make public statements about the importance of faculty self-governance. Board chairs, presidents, and chief academic officers should look for every opportunity to state the importance of effective faculty governance and the faculty's ability to take timely, collective action. At some institutions, faculty governance is ineffective because faculty members believe the hard work of faculty governance is not valued and will make no difference. Frequent public acknowledgements of the role of faculty leaders can help build good will.

On occasion, larger groups of faculty members could be invited to participate in plenary sessions of the board at which academic issues are discussed. For example, if the board is reviewing the report of the chief academic officer concerning changes in expected student-learning outcomes and how to assess those outcomes, it might be helpful to have the chief academic officer and faculty representatives make presentations.

3.2 Encourage faculty governance organizations to be widely representative, including adjunct faculty. If the faculty senate is not representative of the faculty, sharing governance is difficult because faculty-wide engagement will be more difficult. The board could ask whether adjunct faculty and other non-tenure-track faculty members are adequately represented in the faculty senate given their greater role in teaching today. Board members should ask the percentage of courses and student contact hours taught by adjuncts and the percentage of faculty senate positions held by adjuncts. If there is an imbalance, the board and the presidents could ask faculty leaders to consider a change, although, of course, how faculty members govern themselves is determined by the faculty.

3.3 Include faculty leaders in leadership programs. Many faculty members have had no management training and little experience in leadership. They may be in leadership positions merely out of a sense of duty. Too often, academic department chairs are the most recently tenured faculty in the department and the least equipped to exercise true leadership. If there is a leadership program on campus for administrators, seek to include department chairs or faculty senate leaders. If not, consider creating a joint leadership program for both administrators and faculty that will help them take a broader view of the institution, thereby enhancing their capacity for shared governance and perhaps even grooming the next dean, provost, or president. If creating a leadership program is not practical, consider sending faculty leaders to one of the many existing programs or institutes.

Exhibit 8. Suggested Practices for Three-Way Information Sharing

What can the board do?	What can the president do?	What can the CAO and faculty do?
Share board biographies	Shared information about how budgets are built	Share biographies of faculty leaders
Share board committee agendas	Share annual budgets and audit results	Provide summaries of academic actions taken and being considered
Provide summaries of actions taken by the board	Provide a one-page chart describing who makes which decisions	Develop and share a dashboard of indicators relevant to academic quality
Share basic information about board structure	Provide summaries of actions taken by the cabinet and actions under consideration	Share expected student learning outcomes and how outcomes are assessed
Invite faculty leaders to board retreats	Share president's annual goals and objectives	Invite the board chair to speak annually at a faculty meeting or retreat
Involve faculty leaders in board orientations	Include shared governance at board, faculty and staff orientations	Periodically present to the board how important academic decisions (including tenure and promotion) are made
	Educate all about key directional documents, including strategic plans	

3.4 Avoid circumventing faculty leadership. As board members spend more time with faculty members, they are sure to hear from faculty members who express their individual concerns about policies or the direction of the institution. Board members sometimes encourage those faculty members to talk with the president or the chief academic officer about the problem, but they should also encourage them to consult with elected faculty leaders. When board members bring individual faculty concerns to the full board without allowing faculty leaders to consider them, they undercut faculty leadership and hijack time from discussion of collective faculty concerns.

3.5 Reward faculty participation in governance. As discussed in Chapter 4, board members should ask the president and chief academic officer how faculty participation in governance is rewarded. Is it recognized in the tenure and promotion process? Is it considered in determining merit pay? Are faculty members with extraordinary responsibilities in shared governance given release time from other responsibilities or extra compensation? Are they recognized at public events, including commencement?

MAINTAIN A STEADFAST COMMITMENT TO THREE-WAY TRANSPARENCY AND FREQUENT COMMUNICATION

Effective shared governance requires a strong commitment by all parties to transparency, which can allow trust to grow and ease the way to agreement on aligning priorities and responsibilities (see Chapter 2). Exhibit 8 provides some practical suggestions for sharing information with the board, the president, and the faculty.

4.1 Be transparent in communication about information necessary to effectively govern. The board and administration must be transparent with the faculty, providing the information needed to meaningfully and responsibly participate in shared governance. When sharing information with the faculty, chief academic officers must ensure that the information is complete, but they also should be willing to summarize the information for faculty members less willing to dig deeply.

Administrations should be particularly transparent with faculty members about how governance works at the institution (including who makes decisions and how). What are the responsibilities of departments, the faculty senate, other faculty committees, the chief academic officer, the president, the president's cabinet, and the board? Providing faculty members and board members with a shared governance grid similar to Exhibit 9 will be helpful to all involved in the process.

Exhibit 9: Shared Governance Grid

	Board	President	Cabinet	Senior Staff (Specify)	Faculty	Faculty Senate	Faculty Committee (Specify)	Division Chair	Staff Senate	Administrative Committee (Specify)	College Committee	Other (Specify)
Business Oriented Decisions												
Hiring President												
Hiring Vice President												
Strategic Plan												
Campus Master Plan												
Capital Projects												
Institutional Budget												
Student Conduct												
Charter/Bylaws												
Employee Benefits												
President's Goals												
Academically Oriented Decisions												
Hiring Chief Academic Officer												
Curriculum Changes												
New Courses of Study												
Program Closure, No Retrenchment												
Faculty Retrenchment												
Articulation Agreements												
Tenure and Promotion												
Graduation Approval												
Honorary Degrees												
Academic Department Budget												
Faculty Handbook												

Key: **R** = Offers Recommendation, **C** = Consulted, **D** = Makes Decision,
AD = Approves Decision, **HA** = Hears Appeal of Decision

Communication with faculty members by the board and administration must take place early and often. When they are brought into discussions at any point other than the beginning of a decision-making process, they are likely to be suspicious that conclusions have already been drawn or that they are little more than window dressing. (Often board members feel the same way when an overly strong executive committee of the board brings matters to the full board late in the process.)

By the same token, the faculty must also commit to be transparent with the board, particularly with respect to student-learning outcomes. Assessment data, when presented to board academic affairs committees, too often are presented in raw form. Difficulties in understanding the data are compounded when they are partially shrouded in academic or statistical jargon. Efforts by the chief academic officer to develop a data set usable by the board will be much appreciated.

Of course board members can be equally mystified about who makes what decisions at the institution. Most board members, outside of the academic affairs committee, would struggle to describe how curricular decisions are made or how candidates are reviewed for tenure and promotions. And most do not understand the function and role of the faculty senate. Inviting the chief academic officer and the chair of the board's academic affairs committee to conduct a board education session on these topics can be an important element in ensuring a fully informed board.

4.2 Be transparent in budget and other financial matters. Although budget decisions rest primarily with boards, faculty leaders should have a basic understanding of budgets and the opportunity to provide input about priorities, especially academic priorities, before budgets are finalized. Without this understanding of the institution's finances, the faculty are going to be less effective in participating in strategic planning and in understanding the ramifications of decisions regarding future programming and other endeavors.

Many faculty members are not trained to read or understand budgets. And failure to understand the finances of the institution breeds suspicions. Why is the board funding one area and not another? Why is the college building new buildings but tightening departmental budgets or increasing insurance co-pays? Certain best practices in financial information sharing can help:

- Quarterly open forums on budget issues should be organized by the chief financial officer, who can discuss budget matters in ways meaningful to the faculty. It is helpful if the discussion can include how the institution's budget compares with those of peer schools and "stretch schools." At least one of these meetings each year should cover the ABC's of budgeting, how endowments work, and the nature of using restricted funds.

- The president should address budget issues in his or her periodic meetings with faculty. Faculty members expect to hear the president's assessment of financial issues. Especially during difficult economic times, presidents must be candid about financial challenges but, except in extreme situations, should be able to argue that with strong planning and shared responsibility, the institution's financial challenges are not insurmountable.

Explaining Financial Reports

When I was a law school dean at Capital University, I felt that I was fully transparent with the faculty on financial matters because I gave them access to the law school's budget and the university's audit. I would regularly comment on the audit during faculty meetings and ask for questions. I mistook silence for either satisfaction with the law school's and university's finances or trust in the administration to handle the finances appropriately. What I did not then realize was that none of the faculty members attending the faculty meeting had even looked at the audit.

Eventually I decided to simplify matters for them. Believing that one-page summaries were best, I provided the faculty with a dashboard of financial indicators that was concise and nicely set up. But I soon realized that few looked at that, either, because to them it was still a jumble of unfamiliar financial terms and ratios. What the faculty needed was a more nuts-and-bolts approach to understanding financial statements. Thereafter, the law school's chief financial officer held well-attended sessions about the law school's finances. Exposing the faculty to the CFO not only created meaningful transparency but also built trust in the CFO and in the university's financial decision making more generally.

4.4 Ensure a meaningful faculty presence at full board meetings. Even without full board membership, faculty leaders can participate in several ways. One or two elected faculty leaders can be invited to attend board meetings (except executive sessions) as representatives of the faculty and receive the full set of board materials (except those discussed in executive session). When faculty leaders attend board meetings, they should be introduced by the board chair, invited to board dinners and social activities, and asked by the board chair to comment on important matters.

4.5 Routinely include matters of faculty concern in board discussions. This practice helps faculty leaders build credibility with their colleagues. Sometimes faculty members' chief concerns will align with larger trends boards are considering—such as affordability, accessibility, and outcomes. At other times the issues may be more inwardly focused—for example, compensation, faculty morale, levels of faculty staffing, equity in staffing levels. Boards may be inclined to leave such issues to the president, but such issues, particularly at the macro level, are generally fair game for board discussions. For example, discussion of compensation issues—even if it leads to some venting—represents an opportunity for the board to reinforce and the faculty to understand the link between resources and compensation. In addition, the board may learn from faculty how compensation pools could be better allocated between cash compensation and benefits.

Board members can also learn from discussions of faculty concerns what it is like to be a faculty member at their institution and what motivates the faculty. This can be important when the board, for example, is considering new strategic plans that might demand more faculty time, perhaps through greater attention to advising or the need to restructure the curriculum. As boards and the faculty discuss what faculty members might do less of to free up time for new priorities, they will start to think much more strategically about what is most important in these times of challenges to the status quo and what is not as important.

4.6 Have board leaders, the president, and the chief academic officer meet annually with faculty leaders outside of board meetings to allow fuller exchanges of ideas. My own experience is that the very act of the president calling a meeting with faculty and board leaders is a well-appreciated demonstration of confidence in both and can lead to helpfully candid communication.

RESPECT TRADITIONAL RULES OF FACULTY ENGAGEMENT

Until now, this chapter has described the importance of transparency and communication. But successful shared governance is also about the quality of engagement. The quality of the faculty's engagement in important issues is probably the most important factor in whether the faculty develops sufficient ownership of strategic directions to implement them effectively.

The faculty is difficult to engage if the board or administration runs afoul of its traditions and rules of engagement. Boards are tripped up when they fail to understand the importance of process, the best methods of communication, and the rhythm of the academic calendar. Some best practices in this area include the following:

5.1 Recognize that in the eyes of the faculty, process is as important as results. Board members tend to focus on the quality of results, while faculty members tend to focus on the quality of the process (see Chapter 2). When the board and faculty talk about key issues, it is critical to consider the process for framing the discussion and making decisions. For some board members, it can be frustrating to spend a lot of time seeking agreement on the process

On Faculty Morale

Faculty members often raise issues of faculty morale with the board and president, and discussing the issues can be tricky. At times, the discussion comes down to too many expectations, too little communication, and not enough resources. Nonetheless, such a discussion can facilitate an exchange about how to improve the sharing of governance and responsibility. If adeptly handled, the conversation can shift from subjective feelings of happiness or unhappiness to shared plans for developing better systems of communication, better alignment of priorities, and increased faculty engagement. And during difficult times, the best response to low morale is not an inspirational speech or a few dollars applied here or there, but a strong strategic plan. Such plans help the faculty and others understand how they contribute to the success of the institution and how that success will benefit them.

for discussing and making decisions, but it is worth the investment of time to create shared understandings early.

Faculty members tend to ask first whether the right parties have been invited to particular discussions. Decisions of this nature are usually based on custom or tradition at the institution, and the chief academic officer and chair of the faculty senate can be tremendously helpful in this regard. Exhibit 10 can also help sort out some of the issues involved.

In addition to asking who should be at the table, it is important for constituencies to agree on the following elements of good process within the culture of the faculty at the institution:

- **What is the timetable for the discussion?** The desire to reach a mutually agreed upon decision is the best guideline for establishing a timetable, although in some instances the board may set the timetable because of the importance of the decision. The best timetables are usually somewhere between the board's inclinations for speed and the faculty's inclinations for considered deliberation. Some delayed decisions lose their punch, but rushed decisions sometimes have too much punch.

- **What is the process for gathering ideas and input?** More input is better than less to build credibility for the eventual decisions. And the ratio of face-to-face discussion to written statements of opinion should be tipped as much as possible to face-to-face discussion.

- **For data-driven decisions, who gathers the data?** Faculty members, like board members, can be suspicious of data. Are the data representative? Are they complete? Who interprets them? Did the person gathering the data have an agenda? Are the data compared against the most appro-priate benchmark? Most institutions have an institutional research office. This office can be critical to effective decision making if it is viewed as independent. Like the Congressional Budget Office, the institutional research office should be nonpartisan—viewed as independent of both the administration and the faculty.

- **Who ultimately decides?** This must be clear early on to avoid disappointment. The "AGB Statement on Board Accountability," the "AGB Statement on Board Responsibility for the Oversight of Educational Quality," and the AAUP statement referred to in Chapter 3, provide useful guidance for decision making. A summary of who has which responsibilities also can be very helpful (see Exhibit 9).

- **What happens if consensus cannot be reached?** In most cases in which groups are advisory, out of respect for dissenters, it often is appropriate to prepare a minority report. Minority reports do sometimes persuade decisions makers. And even if they do not, they demonstrate respect for dissenters by preserving their views as part of the records of the institution.

5.2 Respect faculty traditions of communication. Faculty members often communicate with each other differently than board members communicate with people in their businesses or in other types of organizations. The best way to communicate with faculty members is not through cross-examination, a lengthy position paper, or a well-reasoned but hard-hitting argument. Rather, it is to understand their culture of communication and adapt accordingly. It is sometimes better to work into an issue somewhat obliquely instead of confronting it head-on in stark terms. If such an approach clearly defines the

---

Exhibit 10. Questions Regarding Who is at the Table When Engaging Faculty

1. For task forces and administrative committee discussions, is the president or provost able to appoint faculty members or are they elected or appointed by faculty leaders?

2. If elected, should the current elected faculty leaders serve or should faculty members be newly elected specifically for the particular discussions?

3. Are tenured members of the faculty the only ones represented?

4. Are part-time and adjunct faculty members adequately represented?

5. Are faculty members from each division, department, or college of the institution to be included?

6. Should representation reflect multicultural diversity?

Meaningful Student Participation in Shared Governance

The "AGB Statement on Board Responsibility for the Oversight of Educational Quality" states that boards should know what students say about the quality of their educational experience, although AGB does not recommend that students serve as voting members of governing boards. Yet the following are among the ways to involve students in shared governance, even if they are "junior partners" in the process:

- Responsible student leaders can be asked to attend board meetings, as guests and not members.

- Student leaders can be appointed to certain board committees, for example search committees for senior administrators, strategic-planning committees, and internal budget advisory committees.

- Student leaders could speak at faculty and board orientations.

- Some presidents appoint a student advisory council to consider a few of the important student-related items the board considers each year and then report their views to the president.

Involving students in a baseline level of shared governance can advance it in a variety of ways:

- There is nothing like individual student testimonials to make reams of data from student surveys come to life.

- Students often have important observations about how to improve student life, academic programs, recruitment, and retention because they are closer to these issues than board members and many faculty members.

- It is helpful to have student advocates who can explain the thinking behind difficult decisions to their peers, either individually, through the student press, or through social media.

The presence of students at the table can aid in focusing all parties on important aspects of our institutions—student learning and achievement. It is easy for boards to get caught up in financial issues, for presidents to be weighed down with day-to-day concerns, and for faculty to focus on the concerns of their academic departments. Students may be future board members, faculty members, and administrators. Involving students in some aspects of governance might inspire some of them to continue their service to their college or university.

issue, it can give faculty members time to get accustomed to the idea (and overcome resistance to even discussing the idea), thus preparing the ground for more direct discussions.

For example, if a board and president are concerned about uneven levels of rigor within certain academic departments, it might be best to ask the chief academic officer and the faculty leaders what learning outcomes are expected from each department and how they are measured. Are these measurements made available to the faculty in the department and across the institution? How are these measures communicated with the board? How can the faculty be sure that there are high expectations in each department? Are departments subjected to periodic outside reviews? Addressing the issue with a series of questions like these can allow faculty leaders to take ownership of the problem and work to suggest possible solutions to any discrepancies among departments.

But at times, with issues that are considered likely to upset at least some faculty members, it is important for presidents and board leaders to acknowledge how faculty members may feel and ask them to provide well-reasoned arguments against the decision that is likely to be made. As noted earlier, deferring a decision because faculty will be upset and grumble gives grumblers a veto. Presidents should invite faculty members into a deeper dialog about their position to try to find a principled middle ground. They can take the same approach to board members who grumble.

CONCLUSION

It's often said that at the core of building effective shared governance is building trust. But in reality, trust is not so much built as it is earned. It takes time and sustained work. And trust that has taken years to build can be squandered in an instant with careless decisions or disrespectful approaches. Boards, faculties, and presidents must consistently commit themselves to building the necessary trust. Fortunately, most leaders of the faculty, board, and administration recognize its importance and will work diligently to engender trust and goodwill.

Conclusion

Clark Kerr, the first Chancellor of the University of California, Berkeley, famously observed in *The Uses of the University* (1962):

> There is a "kind of lawlessness" in any large university, with many separate sources of initiative and power; the task is to keep this lawlessness within reasonable bounds.
>
> The (faculty) groups serve a purpose as a balance wheel— resisting some things that should be resisted, insisting on more thorough discussion of some things that should be more thoroughly discussed, delaying some developments where delay gives time to adjust more gracefully to the inevitable. All this yields a greater sense of order and stability.

Kerr was correct that the difficult task of shared governance can help us all adjust more gracefully to the realities of the present and of the future. This book was designed to help boards, faculties, and administrators to do just that. It is the author's hope that the best practices found in this book will not only help engender better decisions and aligned priorities but also bring more enjoyment to all those engaged in the hard work of college and university governance. After all, there are few greater privileges in life than to serve students and to help them grow, while at the same time helping to ensure healthy futures for the institutions that we all serve.

Appendix: Shared Governance Survey

The first part of the survey assesses the various perspectives on shared governance discussed in Chapter 2. Each person completing the survey should identify which perspective the institution operates under and which it should be operating under. As with the shared governance discussions, this information will aid in developing a "gap analysis" of where the college is, where it wants to be, and how it should get there.

The second part of this survey helps institutions assess the perception of each constituency of the state of shared governance. The result of this section of the survey will yield a treasure trove of information from which to build a basis for better three-way communication among the faculty, the board, and the administration.

Questions to be answered by board members, faculty and administration.

1. Are you a:

☐ tenured faculty member

☐ tenure-track faculty member, not yet tenured

☐ non-tenure track faculty member

☐ board member

☐ administrator

2. Here are four perspectives on shared governance:

A. **Shared governance as equal rights.** Shared governance ensures that faculty, staff and administration have equal say in all governance matters, including budgets, academic directions of the institution and strategic planning. Decisions are not made until a consensus is achieved.

B. **Shared governance as consultation.** Shared governance requires nothing more than for those parties responsible for making decisions to consult with others and consider their positions.

C. **Shared governance as rules of engagement.** Shared governance is a set of rules about the various roles and authority of the board, faculty, and administration in such things as academic decisions, budget decisions, selection of the president, and other decisions. Shared governance also describes rules of engagement when faculty, board members, and administrators disagree, similar to rules set forth by the AAUP.

D. **Shared governance as a system of aligning priorities.** Shared governance is a system of open communication aimed at aligning priorities, creating a culture of shared responsibility for the welfare of the institution, and creating a system of checks and balances to ensure the institution stays mission-centered.

		A	B	C	D
2.1	Which perspective best describes your view of the current state of shared governance at this institution?	☐	☐	☐	☐
2.2	Which perspective best describes what you would like to see with respect to shared governance at this institution?	☐	☐	☐	☐

3. Communication, Transparency, and Respect
To what extent do you agree with the following statements?

		Strongly Disagree	Disagree	Neutral	Agree	Strongly Agree
3.1	Board leaders effectively advocate for shared governance.	☐	☐	☐	☐	☐
3.2	The president and chief academic officer effectively advocate for shared governance.	☐	☐	☐	☐	☐
3.3	Faculty leaders effectively advocate for shared governance.	☐	☐	☐	☐	☐
3.4	The institution enjoys a high degree of transparency with the faculty, by the board.	☐	☐	☐	☐	☐
3.5	The institution enjoys a high degree of transparency with the faculty, by the senior administration.	☐	☐	☐	☐	☐
3.6	Faculty members trust and respect the board.	☐	☐	☐	☐	☐
3.7	Faculty members trust and respect the senior administration.	☐	☐	☐	☐	☐
3.8	The board is adequately informed of the academic program, including desired student outcomes.	☐	☐	☐	☐	☐
3.9	Discussion of difficult matters between the board, faculty and administration are done in good faith and with trust.	☐	☐	☐	☐	☐